"Eloquent and compassionate... *Prison Writings* ...
alongside the best works of ...
Mary Summer Rain, and other ..."
—Douglas ...

"Bill Clinton could go miles ...
freeing Leonard Peltier, whose ...... *Prison Writings* shows
him unbowed despite ...... years in federal prison for a crime he
most likely did not commit."
—*Vanity Fair*

"If you decided that you would only read one book for the rest
of your life, *Prison Writings* should be that book. It is a book that
will move you to stand up against injustice. It will change your
views about life and the lives of future generations."
—*Portland Alliance*

"[*Prison Writings*] will linger on your mind for days...because of
the amazing example of moral strength and dignity exuding
through every single line."
—*Anniston Star*

"Peltier's book...not only offers his persuasive testimony—in
both a civic and a religious sense—but also gives us memorable
glimpses into some of the treasures of his people."
—*Raleigh News and Observer*

"An important contribution to Native American letters, sure to
stir both controversy and renewed attention for Peltier's ongoing
quest for freedom."
—*Kirkus Reviews*

"An inspiring book." —*Library Journal*

"[Leonard Peltier's] simple, eloquent compassion for his captors
as well as himself makes this a remarkable and moving book."
—*Booklist*

"Peltier's book is part of the campaign to gain his freedom, but
also a document of his search for personal peace."
—*Tampa Tribune Times*

"Compelling...[*Prison Writings*] is a lesson in humility and commitment."
—*Oklahoman*

"At long last, we hear Peltier's own voice, coming to us loud and
clear from inside a nightmare world."
—*St. Petersburg Times*

prison

St. Martin's Griffin ᛗ New York

my life
is my
sun dance

writings

leonard peltier

U.S.P. #89637-132

Edited by
Harvey Arden

Introduction by
Chief Arvol Looking Horse

Preface by
Former Attorney General
Ramsey Clark

The photographs printed in this book are gratefully acknowledged in the following order:

p. xii: Leonard Peltier in his cell. Courtesy of Jeffry Scott.

p. 1: Leonard Peltier in his cell. Courtesy of Jeffry Scott.

p. 41: Leonard Peltier in front of his painting of an Indian family. Courtesy of Jeffry Scott.

p. 59: Hawkman II (1992). Courtesy of the Leonard Peltier Defense Committee.

p. 87: Courtesy of Dick Bancroft.

p. 121: Grandma Jumping Bull with family portraits riddled by bullets during the Oglala firefight. Courtesy of Kevin McKiernan, SIPA Press.

p. 137: Under custody of the Royal Canadian Mounted Police. Courtesy of the *Vancouver Sun*.

p. 199: Courtesy of Jeffry Scott.

Preface on page xiii is drawn from Ramsey Clark's speech to the Native American Journalists Association on June 20, 1997.

www.stmartins.com

Library of Congress Cataloging-in-Publication Data

Peltier, Leonard.
    Prison writings : my life is my sun dance / Leonard Peltier; edited by
Harvey Arden ; introduction by Chief Arvol Looking Horse.
        p.   cm.
    ISBN 0-312-20354-3 (hc)
    ISBN 0-312-26380-5 (pbk)
    1. Peltier, Leonard—Imprisonment.   2. Oglala Indians Biography.
3. Indian prisoners—Kansas—Leavenworth Biography.   4. Prisoners'
writings, American—Kansas—Leavenworth.   5. American Indian
Movement.   I. Arden, Harvey.   II. Title.
E99.O3P45   1999
978.1'0049752'0092–dc21
[B]   99-21283
                                                                     CIP

D 30 29 28 27 26 25 24 23 22 21

I would like to thank my adoptive mother, Ethel, and her daughter, Donna, who placed a sweater on my shoulders in the bitter cold of Canada, for thinking of me then as I think of them now. To all my relations who think of me in ceremonies today and tomorrow, your prayers keep me strong because you know the true meaning of *Mitakuye Oyasin*.

*Doing time creates a
demented darkness of my
own imagination. . . .*

*Doing time does this thing
to you. But, of course, you
don't do time.*

*You do without it. Or
rather, time does you.*

*Time is a cannibal that
devours the flesh of your
years*

day by day, bite by bite.

contents

contents

introduction

by Chief Arvol Looking Horse

Hua Kola—

Let it be known that Leonard Peltier is a son of our great grandfathers, a spiritual warrior of the Lakota, Dakota, and Nakota Nations. He shares the spirit of our ancestors who fought for the rights of our people, such as Crazy Horse and Sitting Bull. He is a man who has borne witness to the pain and suffering of our grandmothers, women, and children. As a Sun Dancer, he sacrificed his life to the People seeking justice for all our relatives. He offered himself to Wakan Tanka so that the People might have peace and happiness once again.

I, Chief Arvol Looking Horse, 19th Generation Keeper of the Sacred White Buffalo Calf Pipe, ask that Leonard Peltier receive the blessings of the Great Spirit, for his words to become etched in the minds and hearts of all people. I ask for his prayers to be answered so that he might enjoy the freedom he sought for the People and that the wounds on his soul heal. And I ask those who continue to inflict such pain and suffering on him to see the error of their ways. Let us all work together to restore justice so that the Hoop of Our Nation mends and so our children see better days.

On behalf of all O'yate, I ask Tunkashila for Leonard Peltier to be set free, for him to enjoy his freedom once again. I call on each of you individually and personally, with every breath you take, to never cease in your efforts to free Leonard Peltier. Return him to us!

I, Horse Man, speak these words from my heart, from Paha Sapa, the heart of everything that is — praying for the return of our sacred lands, which have also suffered at the hands of our oppressors.

May peace be with you all.

Mitakuye Oyasin — All My Relations.

Chief Arvol Looking Horse
19th Generation Keeper of the
Sacred White Buffalo Calf Pipe

a prayer

Grandfather,
Mysterious One,
We search for you along
this Great Red Road you have set us on.

Sky Father,
Tunkashila,
We thank you for this world.
We thank you for our own existence.
We ask only for your blessing
and for your instruction.

Grandfather,
Sacred One,
Put our feet on the holy path
that leads to you,
and give us the strength and the will
to lead ourselves and our children
past the darkness we have entered.
Teach us to heal ourselves,
to heal each other
and to heal the world.

Let us begin this very day,
this very hour,
the Great Healing to come.

preface

by Ramsey Clark,
counsel to Leonard Peltier
and former Attorney General
of the United States

I want to tell you why the freedom of Leonard Peltier is so important.

There are well over two hundred million indigenous people on the planet, maybe as many as three hundred million. They live on six continents and on countless numbers of islands. And everywhere they are the most endangered of the human species. Yet *the survival of humanity depends upon their salvation.*

Leonard Peltier is the symbol of that struggle. I am distressed, saddened, and outraged that so many Americans have forgotten, or perhaps never known, who he is and what he represents. If we forget him, we forget the struggle itself. Strangely, he is much better known outside of this country than here—in Europe, in Canada, in South America, in Asia, and Africa. Enlightened people around the world see in him the struggle of all indigenous people for their lives, their dignity, for their sovereignty, their future. And they wonder: how is it that this man has been held so long when his innocence is known by those who hold him? Here in the United States, his voice, and the urgent message of indigenous peoples everywhere, has been muffled if not silenced. Those who put him behind bars—and insist on keeping him there after nearly a quarter century—believe he has been consigned to the dustbin of history, along with the cause of native peoples everywhere. We must not allow that to continue.

I think I can explain beyond serious doubt that Leonard Peltier has committed no crime whatsoever. Even if he had been guilty of firing the gun that killed two FBI agents—and it is certain that he did not—it would still have been in self-defense and in the defense not just of his people but of the right of all individuals and peoples to be free from domination and exploitation. Not a single credible witness said they saw Leonard take aim at anybody that tragic day at Oglala in June 1975 on the Pine Ridge Reservation in South Dakota. There was absolutely no evidence that he killed anyone—except fabricated and utterly misleading circumstantial evidence. Among the many, many things withheld in his alarmingly unfair trial—a trial that disgraced, and continues to disgrace, the American judicial system—was the staggering violence on the Pine Ridge Reservation that led directly to the events of that day. That violence, directed against traditional people on the reservation, had earlier caused the related and better-known tragedy revolving around the occupation and siege at nearby Wounded Knee in 1973. And that violence accelerated enormously in the two years between 1973 and 1975.

At the time of Wounded Knee in 1973, there were only a few FBI agents in the whole state of South Dakota, and frequently just one. But by 1975, there were sixty. They were deployed overwhelmingly against a small Indian population. During those two years more than sixty Indians on the Pine Ridge reservation— some say as many as three hundred—died violent and unexplained deaths, overwhelmingly from activity instigated by our own federal government. And there is little doubt about it.

With government complicity, a rogue paramilitary group that proudly called itself the GOONs— Guardians of the Oglala Nation—were provided with weapons, training, and motivation to create a wave of violence, still remembered as the "reign of terror," against traditional Indian people and their supporters, including the American Indian Movement (AIM). In March of 1975 alone seven Indians were killed, their

deaths going virtually uninvestigated despite the presence of that army of FBI agents and other federal, state,
and tribal lawmen. And that's why the traditional people, the Elders of the Lakota (Sioux) people, asked
AIM, as they had two years before at Wounded Knee,
to send some people to help protect them. And I say,
thank God AIM did.

A small group of brave, dedicated AIM members—
fewer than seventeen people, only six men, Leonard
Peltier among them—came to protect the traditional
Indians from violence secretly and illegally condoned
and initiated by our government. Those AIM defenders, joined by local traditionals, set up a tent city, a
"spiritual camp" they called it, on the remote Pine
Ridge property of Harry and Celia Jumping Bull—two
Elders who feared desperately for their loved ones' lives
after constant threats from the GOONs.

This was a time, we must remember, of government paranoia against all dissident groups that remained as the Vietnam War era was drawing to a close.
These things were all interrelated. We should never
forget Martin Luther King, Jr.'s heartbreaking words in
1967, when he came out against the war in Vietnam
and announced, "The greatest purveyor of violence on
earth is my own government."

There's no question but that our own government
was generating violence against traditional Indians of

Pine Ridge at that time as a means of control and domination, some believe acting on behalf of energy interests planning to purloin the reservation's vast untapped mineral wealth, especially uranium.

We now know, from documents recently released in the 1990s under the Freedom of Information Act, that the FBI had people in place at least twenty minutes before the two cars that precipitated the "incident at Oglala" drove down into the Jumping Bull compound. The government had been preparing for a major act.

During the trial of Leonard Peltier in Fargo, North Dakota, in 1977, much essential background evidence in the case was excluded. The greatest exclusion was all of this government-instigated violence, which had caused the whole tragedy and led to the deaths of their own agents.

Why were these men of AIM there? Why was Leonard Peltier there? He was there to protect people, his own people, who were being killed! If that's a crime, where are we?

But the government's own crimes didn't end there. They suborned our whole system of justice when they intimidated a witness, a poor and unknowing Indian woman, into testifying that she was Leonard Peltier's girlfriend and that she had actually *seen* Leonard kill the agents—then used that testimony to extradite

Leonard from Canada, where he had fled fearing precisely the kind of kangaroo justice he was about to
receive in U.S. courts.

As the FBI well knew, that woman wasn't even
there, had never met or even seen Leonard Peltier,
and the government knew it! It's amazing to me still,
how they talk about that woman and blame her for not
telling the truth. Because, long after it was all over,
they freely admitted "there's not a scintilla of evidence,
not a spark of evidence" — those are their own words —
that this woman was a witness to anything. They admitted she wasn't even there. Now, do you think she
just came forward and volunteered three affidavits?
What did that poor woman go through at the hands of
her interrogators? What type of abuse? It was the same
sort of abuse and manipulation being perpetrated on
the whole traditional population of Pine Ridge — and
by our own government agents. Think of how they
treated her to force her to give utterly false testimony,
and took advantage of her in order to get Leonard
Peltier and bring him back here. What a shameful,
criminal act! So long as it goes unchallenged and un-
punished we are *all* of us, every citizen in this great
nation of ours, subject to the same kind of naked and
arrogant injustice.

The other concealments that the government went
through to imprison Peltier are unbelievable. The FBI

laboratory, as you no doubt have heard, is the subject of a whole series of recent reports that condemn it for fabricating evidence, for falsifying evidence, for incompetence in evaluation of evidence. Yet the extenuated nature of the only evidence against Leonard Peltier is so absurd that, if the FBI laboratory were either competent or honest, that so-called evidence wouldn't be worth anything. The government, in prosecuting its fraudulent case against Leonard, covered up lab reports that said they could not connect the one bullet (it wasn't even a bullet but a casing, an expended casing) with what was called the "Wichita AR-15," the so-called "murder weapon." And yet the FBI claimed to connect the AR-15 bullet casing (itself suspected of being fabricated evidence) with that particular AR-15, even though their own lab said they did not match, and they then illegally concealed this evidence to the contrary throughout Leonard's Fargo trial. Nor, even if they did connect the two, could they place that weapon in Leonard Peltier's hands, much less even prove it to be the "murder weapon." Leonard wasn't within fifteen hundred miles of where it was found near Wichita, Kansas, weeks after the shootout at Oglala. So how does that get to be his rifle in the first place? Well, they had a plan for that. The government argued that there was only one AR-15 rifle possessed by Indians on the reservation. But that was absolutely false, as they well knew. And the courts have since confirmed, without question, that there were a number of AR-15s there, and M-16s as well, which fire the .223 cartridge, which is the same kind of high-velocity cartridge that allegedly killed these FBI agents.

At Leonard's trial, government prosecutors reenacted a scene for which they had no evidence whatsoever — an imaginary scene in which one agent, supposedly suffering from already having been hit at a distance, put his hand in front of his face and begged not to be shot and was shot through the hand and killed by Leonard Peltier, who then whirled and shot the other agent and killed him, both at point-blank range. The only problem was that there was absolutely no evidence of that; no witness testified to anything like that. And yet the jury was intimidated into believing this totally false story.

Then, in 1985, after Leonard had already served a decade in prison, one of the government prosecutors candidly admitted, "We did not know who shot the agents." That's what he said: "We did not know who shot the agents." Now more than another decade has passed and still Leonard Peltier is in prison! He's there, convicted on two counts of murder, and he's serving two life sentences — all for a crime the government *knows* it did not prove he committed! By imprisoning Leonard Peltier, those who keep him locked away from his people continue the government's dishonorable,

centuries-old policy of domination over, and oppression of, Indian peoples. Leonard Peltier is the very
symbol of that domination and continuing oppression.
Is it any wonder he's called a "political prisoner"?

So even after the government admitted that they
did not prove who killed the agents, rather than see
Leonard freed and thus open the door to an investigation into their own misdeeds, they switched after the
fact to a new, equally fraudulent argument for continuing his imprisonment—charging him with "aiding
and abetting" whoever it was who supposedly killed the
agents. Yet the jury had given him a double life sentence because they believed the prosecutor's fabricated
story that Leonard had murdered those injured agents
in cold blood at point-blank range, not for a charge of
"aiding and abetting," which could apply equally to
scores of Indians that day. They would never have
given him a sentence twice his natural life for simply
being at the scene, as were so many, trying to defend
their elders and women and children against the government's unlawful and misguided invasion of the
Jumping Bull property.

The fact is, the government does not have to tell
us who shot the agents. The whole record shows that
officials don't know who shot the agents, and they don't
want anybody else to know. They desperately want the
world to believe that Leonard Peltier is guilty because
they have staked their reputation on it.

preface

The president of the United States can commute that sentence in the name of justice any moment he wants to. He has the power, complete and absolute, under the Constitution. We have to demand that he does it and we must demand that it happens this year, this very day. Each of us and all of us must raise our voices in a chorus of millions, of tens of millions.

Until that happens, every day is a new crime, every dawn is a new crime, every dusk is a new crime against the dignity of the Indian peoples and the honor of the Unites States of America. Because while Leonard Peltier is in prison, we all are.

author's foreword

Innocence is the weakest defense. Innocence has a single voice that can only say over and over again, "I didn't do it." Guilt has a thousand voices, all of them lies.

I have pleaded my innocence for so long now, in so many courts of law, in so many public statements issued through the Leonard Peltier Defense Committee, that I will not argue it here. Nor will I argue the seemingly infinite details of my "case" in these pages. That's been done masterfully well in over six hundred finely detailed pages by Peter Matthiessen in his book *In the Spirit of Crazy Horse: The Story of Leonard Peltier and the FBI's War on the American Indian Movement.* I'm happy to say that brave-hearted book is once again in the stores, after being driven off the counters for some eight years by lawsuits that were ultimately dismissed. The new 1991 edition by Viking/Penguin explains the story of the lawsuits. I'll not dwell on those here, either. I do regret that those lawsuits kept the book away from the public's eye and consciousness precisely at a critical period of my post-trial appeals. I presume that was their intent.

I have issued literally thousands of statements to my supporters over the last twenty years, many of them in *Spirit of Crazy Horse*, the bimonthly journal of the Leonard Peltier Defense Committee. I'm proud that that alternative journal has become an instrument on behalf of justice for many other unjustly held prisoners, not only myself. I'd originally thought that I might simply reprint a selection of my earlier statements to create this book. But, on rereading them, I realized that most of those statements related to the particular circumstances of my case at the time and were so specific to the moment as to be of uncertain relevance today.

Rather than simply edit and reprint my earlier writings, I have asked my friend and longtime supporter Harvey Arden, coauthor of *Wisdomkeepers: Meetings with Native American Spiritual Elders*, to assist me with the demanding task of bringing the whole range of my thoughts and writings into a single focus. While you will find encapsulated herein occasional sentences and even a few paragraphs extracted from my earlier public statements to my supporters, the vast bulk of this book is new, entirely rethought and recrafted.

For Harvey's patient editorial help in this often very difficult process I am immensely grateful. He's insisted that I include not only my public and political thoughts, and fragmentary sketches for an autobiography I hope someday to write—which I'd orginally thought would be enough—but has also prodded me to explore some of my most private feelings and inward experiences, including scraps from a loose-leaf notebook and utterly unorganized collection of journal-like scribblings I've torn from the book of my daily life here in Leavenworth. These have been written down over the months, even years, and have been meshed here with my memories and other thoughts.

What follows in these pages, then, is my own personal testament as best I can set it down under the circumstances. Scattered among those journal entries, soul thoughts, political musings, and personal recollections are nuggets of reflection in the form of poems, but I don't really think of them as poems; they're arrows of meaning, and hopefully of healing, from my heart to yours. I hope they hit their mark. Many of these were written down on scraps of paper in the eternal half-light of my prison nights, and are presented here for the first time. Some seem to me to have a continuing relevance, throwing a few rays of light through the shadows that surround and entangle me. Each catches my frame of mind—and heart—at some crucial moment. In truth, to a man in prison for a crime he didn't commit, every moment is crucial.

Other books and articles pertaining to my case keep coming out, as do films. Best known of the latter has been Robert Redford's and Michael Apted's film documentary *Incident at Oglala*. There's also a major feature film production in the works. I can tell you, from a man who has spent much of his life in a stone-and-steel hole, that I am both immensely grateful for, and utterly amazed at, such attention from an outside world that more often than not forgets those of us within these walls.

To those of us locked away in here, there's nothing more important than being remembered.

Leonard Peltier
September 1998
Leavenworth Prison

part i

in my own voice

This is the twenty-third year

of my imprisonment for a

crime I did not commit.

chapter 1

10:00 P.M. Time for the nightly lockdown and head count. The heavy metal door to my cell lets out an ominous grinding sound, then slides abruptly shut with a loud clang. I hear other doors clanging almost simultaneously down the cellblock. The walls reverberate, as do my nerves. Even though I know it's about to happen, at the sudden noise my skin jumps. I'm always on edge in here, always nervous, always apprehensive. I'd be a fool not to be. You never let your guard down when you live in hell. Every sudden sound has its own terror. Every silence, too. One of those sounds—or one of those silences—could well be my last, I know. But which one? My body twitches slightly at each unexpected footfall, each slamming metal door. Will my death announce itself with a scream or do its work in silence? Will it come slowly or quickly? Does it matter? Wouldn't quick be better than slow, anyway?

A guard's shadow passes by the little rectangular window on the cell door. I hear his keys jangle, and the mindless squawking of his two-way radio. He's peering in, observing, observing. He sees me sitting here cross-legged in the half-light, hunched over on my bed, writing on this pad. I don't look up at him. I can feel his gaze passing over me, pausing, then moving on, pausing again at the sleeping form of my cellmate snoring softly in the bunk above. Now he goes by. The back of my neck creeps.

Another day ends. That's good. But now another night is beginning. And that's bad. The nights are worse. The days just happen to you. The nights you've got to imagine, to conjure up, all by yourself. They're the stuff of your own nightmares. The lights go down but they never quite go out in here. Shadows lurk everywhere. Shadows within shadows. I'm one of those shadows myself. I, Leonard Peltier. Also known in my native country of Great Turtle Island as Gwarth-ee-lass—"He Leads the People." Also known among my Sioux brethren as Tate Wikikuwa—"Wind Chases the Sun." Also known as U.S. Prisoner #89637-132.

I fold my pillow against the cinderblock wall behind me and lean back, half sitting, knees drawn up, here on my prison cot. I've put on my gray prison sweatpants and long-sleeved sweatshirt. They'll do for PJs. It's cool in here this late winter night. There's a shiver in the air. The metal and cinderblock walls and tile floors radiate a perpetual chill this time of year.

Old-timers will tell you how they used to get

thrown, buck naked in winter, into the steel-walled, steel-floored Hole without even so much as a cot or a blanket to keep them warm; they had to crouch on their knees and elbows to minimize contact with the warmth-draining steel floor. Today you generally get clothes and a cot and blanket—though not much else. The Hole—with which I've become well acquainted at several federal institutions these past twenty-three years, having become something of an old-timer myself—remains, in my experience, one of the most inhuman of tortures. A psychological hell. Thankfully, I'm out of there right now.

I'm also out of the heat that used to afflict us until they finally installed air-conditioning in the cellblock about ten years back. Before that Leavenworth was infamous as the Hot House, because there was no air-conditioning here, just big wall-mounted fans that, during the mind-numbing heat of a Kansas hundred-degree summer day, blew the heavy, sluggish, unbreathable air at you like a welding torch, at times literally drying the sweat on your forehead before it could form, particularly on the stifling upper tiers of the five-tier cellblock.

But we still have the noise, always the noise. I suppose the outside world is noisy most of the time, too, but in here every sound is magnified in your mind. The ventilation system roars and rumbles and hisses.

Nameless clanks and creakings, flushings and gurglings sound within the walls. Buzzers and bells grate at your nerves. Disembodied, often unintelligible voices drone and squawk on loudspeakers. Steel doors are forever grinding and slamming, then grinding and slamming again. There's an ever-present background chorus of shouts and yells and calls, demented babblings, crazed screams, ghostlike laughter. Maybe one day you realize one of those voices is your own, and then you really begin to worry.

From time to time they move you around from one cell to another, and that's always a big deal in your life. Your cell is just about all you've got, your only refuge. Like an animal's cage, it's your home—a home that would make anyone envy the homeless. Different cellblocks in this ancient penitentiary have different kinds of cells, some barred, some—like the one I'm currently in—a five-and-a-half-by-nine-foot cinder-block closet with a steel door. There's a toilet and sink, a double bunk bed, a couple of low wall-mounted steel cabinets that provide a makeshift and always cluttered desktop.

Right now they've put another inmate in here with me after I'd gotten used to being blissfully alone for some time. He's got the upper bunk and his inert, snoring form sags down nearly to my head as I try to half sit in here with this legal pad on my lap. At least I get the lower bunk because of the bad knee I've had for

6

years. I presume that they put my new cellmate in here with me as a form of punishment — a punishment for both of us, I suppose — though for what, neither he nor I have the slightest idea.

The first thing you have to understand in here is that you never understand anything in here. For sure, they don't want you ever to get comfortable. Nor do they ever want you to have a sense of security. And, for sure, you don't. Security's the one thing you never get in a maximum-security prison.

Now, on this chilly night, I toss the rough green army blanket over my knees, and drape a hand towel over the back of my neck to keep the chill off. I keep my socks on under the sheets, at least until I finally go to sleep. On this yellow legal pad purchased at the prison commissary I scrawl as best I can with a pencil stub that somebody's been chewing on. I can barely make out my own handwriting in the semidarkness, but no matter.

I don't know if anyone will ever read this. Maybe someone will. If so, that someone can only be you. I try to imagine who you might be and where you might be reading this. Are you comfortable? Do you feel secure? Let me write these words to you, then, personally. I greet you, my friend. Thanks for your time and attention, even your curiosity. Welcome to my world. Welcome to my iron lodge. Welcome to Leavenworth.

chapter 2

I have decided the time has come for me to write, to set forth in words my personal testament — not because I'm planning to die, but because I'm planning to live.

This is the twenty-third year of my imprisonment for a crime I did not commit. I'm now just over fifty-four years old. I've been in here since I was thirty-one. I've been told I must live two lifetimes plus seven years before I get out of prison on my scheduled release date in the year 2041. By then I'll be ninety-seven. I don't think I'll make it.

My life is an extended agony. I feel like I've lived a hundred lifetimes in prison already. And maybe I have. But I'm prepared to live thousands more on behalf of my people. If my imprisonment does nothing more than educate an unknowing and uncaring public about the terrible conditions Native Americans and all indigenous people around the world continue to endure, then my suffering has had — and continues to have — a purpose. My people's struggle to survive inspires my own struggle to survive. Each of us must be a survivor.

I know this. My life has a meaning. I refuse to believe that this existence, our time on Mother Earth, is meaningless. I believe that the Creator, Wakan Tanka, has shaped each of our lives for a reason. I don't know what that reason is. Maybe I'll never know. But you don't have to know the meaning of life to know that life has a meaning.

I acknowledge my inadequacies as a spokesman. I acknowledge my many imperfections as a human being. And yet, as the Elders taught me, speaking out is my first duty, my first obligation to myself and to my people. To speak your mind and heart is Indian Way.

This book is not a plea or a justification. Neither is it an explanation or an apology for the events that overtook my life and many other lives in 1975 and made me unwittingly—and, yes, even unwillingly—a symbol, a focus for the sufferings of my people. But *all* of my people are suffering, so I'm in no way special in that regard.

You must understand. . . . I am ordinary. Painfully ordinary. This isn't modesty. This is fact. Maybe you're ordinary, too. If so, I honor your ordinariness, your humanness, your spirituality. I hope you will honor mine. That ordinariness is our bond, you and I. We are ordinary. We are human. The Creator made us this way. Imperfect. Inadequate. Ordinary.

Be thankful you weren't cursed with perfection. If you were perfect, there'd be nothing for you to achieve with your life. Imperfection is the source of every action. This is both our curse and our blessing as human beings. Our very imperfection makes a holy life possible.

We're not supposed to be perfect. We're supposed to be *useful*.

I realize that I can be moody. That's about all you have left here in prison, your moods. They can gyrate wildly, uncontrollably. You'll find many of those moods in these pages, ranging from near despair to soaring hope, from choking inner rage to everyman's fear and self-doubt. A mood can be overpowering, especially on those days when the endless privations and frustrations of prison life build and build inside me.

And yet, more and more in recent years, I feel detached from it all and strangely free, even within these enclosing walls and razor wire. I credit that to Sun Dance. A man who has Sun Danced has a special compact with Pain. And he'll be hard to break.

Sun Dance makes me strong. Sun Dance takes place inside of me, not outside of me. I pierce the flesh of my being. I offer my flesh to the Great Spirit, the Great Mystery, Wakan Tanka. To give your flesh to

10

Spirit is to give your life. And what you have given you can no longer lose. Sun Dance is our religion, our strength. We take great pride in that strength, which enables us to resist pain, torture, any trial rather than betray the People. That's why, in the past, when the enemy tortured us with knives, bullwhips, even fire, we were able to withstand the pain. That strength still exists among us.

When you give your flesh, when you're pierced in Sun Dance, you feel every bit of that pain, every iota. Not one jot is spared you. And yet there is a separation, a detachment, a greater mind that you become part of, so that you both feel the pain and see yourself feeling the pain. And then, somehow, the pain becomes contained, limited. As the white-hot sun pours molten through your eyes into your inner being, as the skewers implanted in your chest pull and yank and rip at your screaming flesh, a strange and powerful lucidity gradually expands within your mind. The pain explodes into a bright white light, into revelation. You are given a wordless vision of what it is to be in touch with all Being and all beings.

And for the rest of your life, once you have made that sacrifice of your flesh to the Great Mystery, you will never forget that greater reality of which we are each an intimate and essential part and which holds each of us in an embrace as loving as a mother's arms.

11

Every time a pin pricks your finger from then on, that little pain will be but a tiny reminder of that larger pain and of the still greater reality that exists within each of us, an infinite realm beyond reach of all pain. There even the most pitiable prisoner can find solace.

So Sun Dance made even prison life sustainable for me.

I am undestroyed.

My life is my Sun Dance.

chapter 3

I have no apologies, only sorrow. I can't apologize for
what I haven't done. But I can grieve, and I do. Every
day, every hour, I grieve for those who died at the
Oglala firefight in 1975 and for their families—for the
families of FBI agents Jack Coler and Ronald Williams
and, yes, for the family of Joe Killsright Stuntz—whose
death from a bullet at Oglala that same day, like the
deaths of hundreds of other Indians at Pine Ridge at
that terrible time, has never been investigated. My
heart aches in remembering the suffering and fear under which so many of my people were forced to live
at that time, the very suffering and fear that brought
me and the others to Oglala that day—to defend the
defenseless.

And I'm filled with an aching sorrow, too, for the
loss to my own family because, in a very real way, I
also died that day. I died to my family, to my children,
to my grandchildren, to myself. I've lived out my death
for more than two decades now.

Those who put me here and keep me here knowing of my innocence can take grim satisfaction in their sure reward—which is being who and what they are. That's as terrible a reward as any I could imagine.

I know who and what I am. I am an Indian—an Indian who dared to stand up to defend his people. I am an innocent man who never murdered anyone nor wanted to. And, yes, I am a Sun Dancer. That, too, is my identity. If I am to suffer as a symbol of my people, then I suffer proudly.

I will never yield.

If you, the loved ones of the agents who died at the Jumping Bull property that day, get some salve of satisfaction out of my being here, then at least I can give you that, even though innocent of their blood. I feel your loss as my own. Like you, I suffer that loss every day, every hour. And so does my family. We, too, know that inconsolable grief. We Indians are born, we live, and we die with inconsolable grief. We've shared our common grief for twenty-three years now, your families and mine, so how can we possibly be enemies? Perhaps it's with *you* and with *us* that the healing can start. You, the agents' families, certainly weren't at fault that day in 1975, any more than my family was, and yet you and they have suffered as much as, even more than, anyone there. It seems it's always the innocent who

14

pay the highest price for injustice. It's seemed that way all my life.

To the still-grieving Coler and Williams families I send my prayers if you will have them. I hope you will. They are the prayers of an entire people, not just my own. We have many dead of our own to pray for, and we join our sorrow to yours. Let our common grief be our bond. Let those prayers be the balm for your sorrow, not an innocent man's continued imprisonment. I state to you absolutely that, if I could possibly have prevented what happened that day, your menfolk would not have died. I would have died myself before knowingly permitting what happened to happen. And I certainly never pulled the trigger that did it. May the Creator strike me dead this moment if I lie. I cannot see how my being here, torn from my own grandchildren, can possibly mend your loss. I swear to you, I am guilty only of being an Indian. That's why I'm here.

Being who I am, being who you are—that's Aboriginal Sin.

aboriginal sin

We each begin in innocence.
We all become guilty.
In this life you find yourself guilty
    of being who you are.
Being yourself, that's Aboriginal Sin,
the worst sin of all.
That's a sin you'll never be forgiven for.

We Indians are all guilty,
guilty of being ourselves.
We're taught that guilt from the day we're born.
We learn it well.

To each of my brothers and sisters, I say,
be proud of that guilt.
You are guilty only of being innocent,
of being yourselves,
of being Indian,
of being human.

Your guilt makes you holy.

16

chapter 4

The death of loved ones is harder to take than your own. Your own death is easy by comparison. When I wasn't allowed to attend my father's funeral in 1989, I suffered pain worse than any physical pain. Pain without hope of closure, a wound eternally unhealed. He'd seen his son falsely imprisoned for fourteen years, and it broke his heart. He'd served in World War II, getting machined-gunned in the legs for his effort; his brother, my uncle Ernie, was killed in battle. You'd think the government he'd risked his life to defend might at least allow his son to attend his funeral, but no way. Vengeance runs deep.

And there have been so many other deaths of close ones and supporters just these past few years: the death of Hazel Little Hawk, my spiritual mother who was friend to so many for so many years; Uncle Louie Irwin, a warrior with a heart as strong as a bear's, who inspired me every day and helped me to survive in this nightmare place as my friend, supporter, and advisor; my selfless legal counselor and friend Lew Gurwitz; and all too many others.

I think of all those who have died violently along the same Red Road I've walked: Joe Killsright Stuntz, killed by an unknown assailant's bullet at Oglala. Dallas Thundershield, shot down during our escape attempt from Lompoc, which I'll deal with later on, and Bobby Garcia, our fellow escapee, found unaccountably dead in his cell a couple of years later. There was Anna Mae Aquash, my wonderful Micmac sister in AIM—scheduled to be a defense witness in my Fargo trial—who was murdered in South Dakota for being innocent and being Indian, her hands cut off by a vengeful FBI and sent to Washington for identification when they knew very well who she was. That was a desecration deliberate and calculated, an assault on our deepest and most intimate spiritual beliefs, intended to intimidate us at the very core of our being.

When the feds threatened another poor Indian woman, Myrtle Poor Bear, that they would do the same thing to her and her child if she didn't testify falsely against me, she so testified. Later she recanted the story prosecutors had fabricated for her, though it had already done me in. Now, *her* I can understand and even perhaps forgive. But those who, for a few pieces of U.S. silver or for whatever misguided motives, inflicted this evil on this poor woman and on me and on *all* of us, including the American people themselves . . . I often wonder what fitful dreams come to them at night if they truly believe in their Christian God and the eternal sizzling hell that surely lies waiting for them.

But . . . no . . . there I go, being vindictive and vengeful myself, wishing harm on others as they have wished it on me. I have to watch that in myself. I have to step on the head of that snake every time it rises. There's always someone to hate. The list of those who have earned our hatred — and spurned our hatred — is endless. Shall we draw up lists of each other's crimes? Must we hate each other for all time?

I know I have often spoken out against Indian people who, it seemed to us, stood with the oppressors, turning against their own people. But, I know, that's an oversimplification. Indians have no easy choices. I see now that the U.S. Secret Service — none less — is advertising for recruits in an Indian newspaper. Imagine that! And I know, too, that there are good-hearted Native people in the FBI, devoted, dedicated, loyal, good Americans as they are good Indians. They've made that choice, and though I may not agree with it, I do respect it. I know the strain upon their hearts. It's good you're there, my brothers and sisters . . . so they can see us for what we are, human beings, yes, ordinary — and extraordinary — human beings. Just the same as all other human beings on this earth.

Yes, even we prisoners are human.

I suppose every man proclaims himself innocent, whether innocent or not.

But, I tell you, even the guilty are human. And, as for the innocent who are branded as guilty, theirs is a special agony beyond all comprehension.

Somehow Wakan Tanka, Tunkashila, the Great Mystery, finds sense and meaning in all of this.

Do the stars have a meaning? Then my life has a meaning.

No doubt my name will soon be among the list of our Indian dead. At least I will have good company—for no finer, kinder, braver, wiser, worthier men and women have ever walked this earth than those who have already died for being Indian.

Our dead keep coming at us, a long, long line of dead, ever growing and never ending. To list all their names would be impossible, for the great, great majority of us have died unknown, unacknowledged. Yes, even our dead have been stolen from us, uprooted from our memory just as the bones of our honored ancestors have been dishonored by being dug up from their graves and shipped to museums to be boxed and catalogued and hidden away in file drawers, denied that final request and right of every human being: a decent burial in Mother Earth and proper ceremonies of remembrance to light the way to the afterworld.

20

Yes, the roll call of our Indian dead needs to be cried out, to be shouted from every hilltop in order to shatter the terrible silence that tries to erase the fact that we ever existed.

I would like to see a red stone wall like the black stone wall of the Vietnam War Memorial, which I've only seen in pictures. Yes, right there on the Mall in Washington, D.C. And on that red stone wall — pigmented with the living blood of our people (and I would happily be the first to donate that blood) — would be the names of all the Indians who ever died for being Indian. It would be hundreds of times longer than the Vietnam Memorial, which celebrates the deaths of fewer than sixty thousand brave lost souls. The number of our brave lost souls reaches into the many millions, and every one of them remains unquiet until this day. Just as effective might be a Holocaust Museum to the American Indian to recall the voices of those who were slaughtered.

Yes, the voices of Sitting Bull and Crazy Horse, of Buddy Lamont and Frank Clearwater, of Joe Stuntz and Dallas Thundershield, of Wesley Bad Heart Bull and Raymond Yellow Thunder, of Bobby Garcia and Anna Mae Aquash . . . those and so, so many others. Their stilled voices cry out at us and demand to be heard.

My life is a prayer for my people.

chapter 5

I've been treated no worse than many other prisoners; better than some. At least I'm alive. Recently, for some unexplained reason, they confiscated the ceremonial skirt towel I've used for years in our sacred sweat lodge; they tell me it's been thrown away. That hurt more than the physical deprivations and the bouts of solitary confinement.

The beatings, by and large, have stopped—I hope. I've been beaten in the past for the high crime of passing half a sandwich to another inmate—I'd have eaten it myself but my jaw was too swollen, so instead of seeing it thrown away, I gave it to another guy who was hungry. That got me two bruised ribs and an even sorer jaw than usual, and my headaches were even worse for a while from a bang my head took against the corner of a door frame.

I have terrible headaches much of the time. I lost 80 percent of the vision in my left eye from a retinal hemorrhage I suffered years ago. I'm also told I've tested positive for hepatitis B. I've been forced to work in the prison furniture factory, despite my chronic ill health.

My mouth is a horror show; as a kid I had lockjaw, and my bite and gums have never been right since. I also had a break in my jaw that never healed correctly. My jaw is swollen and gives me constant pain. I've had three unsuccessful jaw surgeries in prison facilities in recent years.

The doctors at the Springfield, Missouri, federal prisoners medical facility where I was treated could not agree on a treatment for my jaw. One wanted to put a drainage tube on the outside of my mouth, the other a drainage tube on the inside. Each said that the other didn't know what he was talking about. In one operation they put plastic joints in my jaw, and then one of the joints came loose and fell out, and for weeks I had loose wires sticking out of my jaw on the inside, scraping my tongue and gums and inner cheek raw.

Though my jaw remained—and still remains—locked almost completely shut, with only a narrow slit between my teeth through which soft mashed food can be pushed, I have been refused special food. "Eat applesauce, it's good for you," I was told by one guard with a sneering smile. Throughout most of my stays at Springfield I was held not in the hospital but in a segregated punishment cell crawling with ants, lice, and cockroaches. At the last operation I lost so much blood that repeated transfusions were required. I can tell you, I passed to the other world during that time; I was sure I had died and I was glad it was finally over. I was looking forward to joining all those friends and relatives who had passed to the Sky World before me — and then I was suddenly back in my filthy cell at Springfield. For some reason I was also given prolonged radiation treatments, though I've been told by outside doctors that there's absolutely no reason to use radiation in cases like mine.

I've refused further prison surgery and requested immediate medical treatment by an independent specialist; that request is still being denied. Some of my supporters worried I was being deliberately bled or radiated to death by vengeful authorities. I think not. Death would have been bliss compared to that, in any case, and they certainly don't want me to know bliss of any kind.

When the pain screaming in my jaw gets too bad, I just close my eyes and think of Sun Dance. That helps. My body may be locked in here, but my spirit flies with the eagle.

the heart of the world

Here I am,
locked in my own shadow
    for more than twenty years,
and yet
I have reached my hand
    through stone and steel and razor wire
and touched the heart of the world.
Mitakuye Oyasin, *my Lakota brethren say.*
We are all related.
We are One.

in the shadowed night

Sometimes
in the shadowed night
I become spirit.
The walls, the bars, the gratings dissolve into light
and I unloose my soul
and fly through the inner darkness of my being.
I become transparent,
a bright shadow,
a bird of dreams singing from the tree of life.

chapter 6

You never get used to prison life. In my sleep I hear people's voices, some of them long dead, like my father. Such voices are torture. To wonder every day, every hour, whether or not you will *ever* be free again is a very special form of torture. It takes its daily, hourly toll on your heart and in your soul, particularly when you have to explain to your grandson why they won't let you out to attend his soccer game. It eats you up inside to hear his little boy's voice ask, "Grandpa, why don't you just *finish* your sentence?" He thought my sentence was just a whole lot of words I had to write, like copying a sentence over and over for a punishment assignment at his grade school. He couldn't understand that my sentence continues for twice my natural life.

When, on their occasional visits in here, I hold my grandchildren in my arms and smell the scent of their hair and feel the warmth of their little hands in my own, I am momentarily transported. But then comes the inevitable clang of the metal doors sliding shut behind them as they leave, and I'm transported instantly back here, to this eternal iron lodge called Leavenworth. That metallic clanging echoes in my soul as it reverberates down the cold-walled corridors.

In all honesty, I can tell you that I wish I hadn't been at the Jumping Bull camp that day in 1975. But I've never regretted that I was one of those who stood up and helped to protect my people. I've sacrificed nearly a quarter century of my life, of my freedom, for so standing up. I admit it, I'm tired. Over the years, I've hidden away my suffering. I smile when I feel like crying. I laugh when I feel like dying. I have to stare at pictures of my children and my grandchildren to see them grow up. I miss the simplest things of ordinary life—having dinner with friends, taking walks in the woods. I miss gardening. I miss children's laughter. I miss dogs barking. I miss the feel of the rain on my face. I miss babies. I miss the sound of birds singing and of women laughing. I miss winter and summer and spring and fall. Yes, I miss my freedom. So would you.

One of our great Lakota spiritual elders, the late Mathew King, said: "Only one thing's sadder than remembering you once were free, and that's *forgetting* you once were free. That would be the saddest thing of all."

That's something I, Leonard Peltier, will never do.

I will never forget the taste of freedom.

Nor will I forget the sight of the sunrise or the sunset. One day I hope to see those again.

One morning you wake up and you find you've been given something you didn't want . . . two life sentences plus seven years. These gray-green steel gratings, these cold cement walls, these endless coils of razor wire, these sliding steel doors that take you from nowhere to nowhere, these shadowed and inhuman corridors are now your world. This place is yours, they tell you, until the year 2041. Not one lifetime sentence but two. Consecutive. That plus seven years, of course — that's for once, in 1978, having tried to escape to avoid being assassinated, which I will cover later.

I tell myself: Be thankful you didn't get *three* lifetime sentences, Leonard. After all, you could have *not* killed three people instead of *not* killing two! They'd really have thrown the book at you then! Yes, Leonard, consider two lifetimes plus seven years very, very lenient for the high crime of being innocent.

There's no telling how long I'll actually be here. Once I counted in days, then weeks, then months, then years. Now I count in decades. I've already done two decades. Must I do two more? Three? Four? Seems the arithmetic gets easier as the time gets harder.

30

. . .

You can have mad thoughts in here. Like . . . tell me, when I die, do they bring my corpse back to my cell to serve out the full term of my second sentence plus those seven years? Perhaps I've already been brought back and have just forgotten it? Maybe I'm already a corpse? A breathing cadaver? But no, no. A cadaver couldn't smile at himself this way. Somewhere, somehow, there's got to be something funny about all of this. Something horrendously funny. A wild cosmic joke on me, a real knee-slapper in some demonic heaven or hell.

A while back someone was crying out eerily down the corridor in the echoing half-darkness. *"Slur the buds!"* he cried out dementedly, repeating those meaningless words over and over again in a ghostly voice, softly hissing and hollow. *"Slur the buds! Slur the buds!"* That's all I could make out. He must have called it out in that soft hollow hiss a dozen times in the course of fifteen minutes. Still other voices picked it up, and for a short while there was an impromptu ghostly chorus of *"Slur the buds!"* echoing down these unholy corridors.

I never learned what the words meant. I never learned who it was who called out. Maybe I dreamed it. Maybe that was just me myself calling out in the demented darkness of my own imagination.

Doing time does this thing to you. But, of course, you don't do time. You do without it. Or rather, time does you. Time is a cannibal that devours the flesh of your years day by day, bite by bite. And as he finishes the last morsel, with the juices of your life running down his bloody chin, he smiles wickedly, belches with satisfaction, and hisses out in ghostly tones, *"Slur the buds!"*

the knife of my mind

I have no present.
I have only a past
and, perhaps, a future.
The present has been taken from me.

I'm left in an empty space whose darkness
I carve at with the knife of my mind.
I must carve myself anew
out of the razor-wire nothingness.

I will know the ecstasy
and the pain
of freedom.
I will be ordinary again.
Yes, ordinary,
that terrifying condition,
where all is possibility,
where the present exists and must be faced.

chapter 7

On a windowsill beyond the bars a pigeon stands on pink feet, chest fluffed out, preening in the morning sun. Some paint has peeled off the painted-over window, and, pressing my forehead right up against the cold glass, I peek out at him sitting there, a universe away. The pigeon doesn't see me staring at him. His feathers have a subtle iridescence to them. The hand of my mind reaches out and touches him through the bars and the thick security glass. A spirit touch. He doesn't seem to notice. He pecks his small sharp beak into those iridescent chest feathers and ignores me.

I marvel at the miracle of him, standing there, so near yet far, unfettered as the wind. The whole sky is his, and yet from all that infinite space he's picked this bleak prison windowsill to pause upon this winter morning, blessing me with his sudden unexpected presence, his astonishing reality.

To me, the jailbird, this pigeon is as holy a messenger as an eagle. He tells me of the Sky World beyond the steel and cement and razor wire. Once, when we came out of the prison sweat lodge, we looked up and saw two eagles circling high above us. They came to bless us, sent by Sky Father.

So I am known to the eagle and to the pigeon, holy messengers both. Sky Father hasn't forgotten me. He sends his winged children to comfort me.

And I send skyward through the bars a winged prayer of thanks.

No prison bars can stop a prayer.

chapter 8

Many nights I lie here in my bunk and let my mind, my dreams, flow free, conjuring up a future I may never see. Certainly I pray my long journey doesn't end behind prison bars. I know it will not. My Cree brethren in Canada say they've set aside a parcel of land for me where I can raise a small herd of sacred buffalo. I dream of that often. But then I think to myself: Leonard, that's just selfishness, to go off and live the good life and forget the struggle. Yes, of course, I have some living to catch up on when I get out of here, but my life will still be my people's.

When at last I'm a free man again, the real work will begin. Our most important work, before all else, is our survival as a people. This means we must work unceasingly, no matter what the odds, for the honoring of the treaties. We must never lose sight of that. I fear that Indian people will lose what culture we have left, that we will lose our land base, that those who would drive us off our territories into nonexistence will succeed. Our vigilance and our total determination in this regard must never let up. No, not ever.

But within that greater struggle, we must turn and help ourselves and our people, one by one. There's not a one of us who can't give a helping hand, just as there's not a one of us who can't benefit from a helping hand. We must reach out helping hands to each other.

Prison hasn't prevented me from helping people. I organize clothing, food, and toy drives year round. I support women's shelters and Head Start programs. I have established a scholarship for Native law students at New York University and also helped to fund a newspaper by and for Indian children. I'm a foster parent to two young boys in Guatemala and El Salvador. I've been working on ways to improve the health care system on the Rosebud Reservation, and recently have become involved in economic reform for Pine Ridge. I've just recently sponsored a drive, in conjunction with Food Not Bombs, to buy rice, beans, sugar, and other staples for our struggling Indian brothers and sisters now fighting for their very existence, their very identity as Indian people, down in Chiapas, Mexico. I work closely with the Leonard Peltier Charitable Foundation, devoted to helping underprivileged Indian children. I'm also deeply involved in winning Native religious rights here in prison, a continuous battle. Still, I'm limited in what I can do within these walls.

My dream is to rejoin the people and build Native American community centers offering after-school activities and counseling. I want to work with specialists from around the world to help prevent and treat alcoholism. I want to help create jobs and job training for Indian people. It's so frustrating to hear over and over again about teen suicide, drug abuse, unemployment, and seemingly eternal poverty among my people. I ask myself, what has my sacrifice been for?

And yet I know when this sacrifice ends, a new sacrifice begins. There's always another Sun Dance.

i am everyone

I am everyone
who ever died
without a voice
or a prayer
or a hope
or a chance . . .
everyone who ever suffered
for being an Indian,
for being human,
for being indigenous,
for being free,
for being Other,
for being committed. . . .

I am every one of them.
Every single one.
Yes.
Even you.

I am everyone.

part ii

who i am

I am an Indian man. My

only desire is to live like one.

chapter 3

My life is an Indian life. I'm a small part of a much larger story. If I ever have the years of freedom necessary to write another book, I'll appear in it only as a minor character. The personal specifics of my life are unimportant. Being an Indian, that's what's important. My autobiography is the story of my people, the Indian people of this Great Turtle Island. My life has meaning only in relation to them. It's insignificant in and of itself. Only when I identify with my people do I cease being a mere statistic, a meaningless number, and become a human being.

American Indians share a magnificent history — rich in its astounding diversity, its integrity, its spirituality, its ongoing unique culture and dynamic tradition. It's also rich, I'm saddened to say, in tragedy, deceit, and genocide. Our sovereignty, our nationhood, our very identity — along with our sacred lands — have been stolen from us in one of the great thefts of human history. And I am referring not just to the thefts of previous centuries but to the great thefts that are still being perpetrated upon us today, at this very moment. Our human rights as indigenous peoples are being violated every day of our lives—and by the very same people who loudly and sanctimoniously proclaim to other nations the moral necessity of such rights.

Over the centuries our sacred lands have been repeatedly and routinely stolen from us by the governments and peoples of the United States and Canada. They callously pushed us onto remote reservations on what they thought was worthless wasteland, trying to sweep us under the rug of history. But today, that so-called wasteland has surprisingly become enormously valuable as the relentless technology of white society continues its determined assault on Mother Earth. White society would now like to terminate us as peoples and push us off our reservations so they can steal our remaining mineral and oil resources. It's nothing new for them to steal from nonwhite peoples. When the oppressors succeed with their illegal thefts and depredations, it's called colonialism. When their efforts to colonize indigenous peoples are met with resistance or anything but abject surrender, it's called war. When the colonized peoples attempt to resist their oppression and defend themselves, we're called criminals.

I write this book to bring about a greater understanding of what being an Indian means, of who we are as human beings. We're not quaint curiosities or stereotypical figures in a movie, but ordinary—and, yes, at times, extraordinary—human beings. Just like you. We feel. We bleed. We are born. We die. We aren't stuffed dummies in front of a souvenir shop; we aren't sports mascots for teams like the Redskins or the Indians or the Braves or a thousand others who steal and distort and ridicule our likeness. Imagine if they called their teams the Washington Whiteskins or the Washington Blackskins! *Then* you'd see a protest! With all else that's been taken from us, we ask that you leave us our name, our self-respect, our sense of belonging to the great human family of which we are all part.

Our voice, our collective voice, our eagle's cry, is just beginning to be heard. We call out to all of humanity. Hear us!

chapter 10

Often I see Indians fighting Indians, badmouthing each other and worse. My white friends ask me, "Why can't you Indians get together and act in unison?"

Why? Do white people speak with one voice on all issues? Why should *we*? Should Indians be under some form of dictatorship that would keep us all in line? That's precisely what we're trying to avoid. We can't give up our freedom in order to keep our freedom! We will assure our own survival only by acting as free men and free women—which we are. Free, at least, in our minds and in our hearts and in our dreams, even if our bodies are shackled and locked away.

We each speak our piece; that's our duty to our people. That's why each of us is a leader. That's Indian Way. *That's* true democracy, not a dictatorship of the elite and powerful who get themselves elected and then make secret deals on their own behalf behind the people's backs. They have no beliefs, such people, but their own selfish interests. They care nothing for others or for the Earth or for the Seventh Generation. We oppose such people and the system they have created by and for themselves. We believe many, many among you, peoples of all races and nations, join us in this opposition. We ask, we *demand*, that our voices be heard in the councils of humanity. Someone *must* speak for the Earth and the Seventh Generation! There should be delegations of indigenous people at every national congress and at every international conference. We are the voices of the earth. We speak for those who are not yet born. When you exclude us, you exclude your own conscience. We *are* your conscience!

an eagle's cry

Listen to me!
Listen!
I am the Indian voice.
Hear me crying out of the wind,
Hear me crying out of the silence.
I am the Indian voice.
Listen to me!

I speak for our ancestors.
They cry out to you from the unstill grave.
I speak for the children yet unborn.
They cry out to you from the unspoken silence.

I am the Indian voice.
Listen to me!
I am a chorus of millions.
Hear us!
Our eagle cry will not be stilled!

We are your own conscience calling to you.
We are you yourself
crying unheard within you.

48

Let my unheard voice be heard.
Let me speak in my heart and the words be heard
whispering on the wind to millions,
to all who care,
to all with ears to hear
and hearts to beat as one
with mine.

Put your ear to the earth,
and hear my heart beating there.
Put your ear to the wind
and hear me speaking there.

We are the voice of the earth,
of the future,
of the Mystery.

Hear us!

chapter 11

My own personal story can't be told, even in this ab-
breviated version, without going back long before my
own birth on September 12, 1944, back to 1890 and to
1876 and to 1868 and to 1851 and, yes, all the way back
through all the other calamitous dates in the relations
between red men and white, back to that darkest day
of all in human history: October 12, 1492, when our
Great Sorrow began.

But, for our limited purposes in these pages, let's
skip past all those earlier dates and settle here for beginning my story in 1890, that crucial and terrible year,
the year when we and the Sacred Hoop of our Nation
were finally broken.

Or so they thought.

Whenever I think of the holocaust that occurred at
Wounded Knee, South Dakota, on December 29,
1890, I hear the voices of the children crying out from
the cold and hunger and terror. I hear the wails and

lamentations of the mothers weeping in agony for their dying babies.

The stories passed on to me by the Lakota Elders describe the incredible sufferings of Chief Big Foot and his starving followers as they fled through the vicious Dakota winter on their way to Pine Ridge that terrible December day, just two weeks after the utterly unprovoked murder of Sitting Bull, who was murdered through treachery like so many others of our people.

Big Foot's band, fleeing for their lives, didn't know why they were being targeted and killed; they were heading for refuge with Red Cloud's band at Pine Ridge. Ostensibly, claimed the government, they sent their troops to stop us from performing the Ghost Dance, a purely religious rite. This was just a pretext, of course; they're very good to this day at finding pretexts to attack us. The real reason behind their attack was that they wanted to run their railroads from the stolen Black Hills back to Chicago and the East, right through what was left of our lands, which the Fort Laramie Treaty of 1868 had solemnly promised to us for "as long as the grass grows and the rivers run."

When Big Foot's starving, freezing band saw the soldiers of the Seventh Cavalry, Custer's old unit, moving toward them through the deep snow, they figured the cavalry could only be there to help them, surely. Hadn't they been told that if they surrendered to the

Indian Agency at Pine Ridge they would be cared for with food and medicine and shelter?

I can physically feel this very moment the misery and suffering that more than three hundred men, women, and children endured as they made their way through South Dakota blizzards, below-zero temperatures, and impenetrable snowdrifts. I can imagine the terror and the fear rushing through them as the soldiers opened fire on them the following morning—the echoes and roar of the Gatling guns mixed with booming cannons and the rattling sabers and the screams of the women and children.

As an Indian of Sioux blood I can hear those screams and feel the pain of those mothers, children, and old men as they are torn to pieces by the bullets and the flashing blood-tipped sabers, striking them again and again and again as they lay there defenseless. I relive every one of their deaths. I die with each one of them again and again.

Chief Big Foot's band had refused to fight the *wasichu* (white man), believing only peace could overcome the animosity between the people. Big Foot himself was an old man at the time, nearly dead of pneumonia. They surrendered to the cavalry, camped at Wounded Knee Creek, ate a meager meal—much like the final meal of the condemned before execution—slept a few hours, and then that next morning were promptly slaughtered, allegedly because one old Indian, probably deaf, had raised his rifle rather than surrender it to a soldier. Somehow the gun went off—or so the government claimed—and the Gatling guns and cannons up on the hill fired right down into the people. They even killed a few dozen of their own soldiers standing there.

Afterward, the proud butchers of the Seventh Cavalry were awarded twenty-six Medals of Honor for their heroics. White man's history books still call it a "battle," as if to give some dignity to what had none. It was a slaughter, pure and simple. A crime against all humanity, though there was no such phrase in those days.

The late James High Hawk, one of the few survivors of the Wounded Knee massacre, gave this eyewitness account:

My mother was crying and trying to save and protect her small family, and I was myself just a little boy. A soldier came to where we were hiding and shot my mother and baby brother and myself as my mother pleaded for our lives. I was wounded and lay there for hours, until Oglalas [Lakotas] from Pine Ridge saved me.

. . . This massacre is . . . the most disgraceful, cowardly, and treacherous killing ever staged by the United States Army. White people say the Indians are treacherous, but we are not. We love our families. We do not bother the white people, but they came here and killed us—women and children. We have the wounds to prove what they've done.

Yes, we have the wounds. And these atrocities against my people continue to this day, only now they're carried out with more sophisticated means than Gatling guns and cannons and sabers. There are subtler ways of killing. Call it death by statistics. Today, white man lets his statistics do the killing for him. Indian reservations in South Dakota have the highest rates of poverty and unemployment and the highest rates of infant mortality and teenage suicide, along with the lowest standard of living and the lowest life expectancy—barely forty years!—in the country. Those statistics amount to genocide. Genocide also disguises itself in the form of poor health facilities and wretched housing and inadequate schooling and rampant corruption. Our remaining lands, eyed by a thousand local schemers only too eager to stir up trouble and division on the reservation, continue to be sold off acre by acre to pay off tribal and individual debts. No square inch of our ever-shrinking territory seems beyond the greedy designs of those who would drive us into nonexistence.

The American Indian Movement through the

years has sought every means possible to bring these crimes against humanity to the attention of the world, hoping that at least some of you would listen and search deep within yourselves for the humanity to demand that the U.S. government stop these crimes.

The destruction of our people must stop!

We are not statistics. We are the people from whom you took this land by force and blood and lies. We are the people to whom you promised to pay, in recompense for all this vast continent you stole, some small pitiful pittance to assure at least our bare survival. And we are the people from whom you now snatch away even that pittance, abandoning us and your own honor without a qualm, even launching military attacks on our women and children and Elders, and targeting—illegally even by your own self-serving laws—those of us, our remaining warriors, who would dare to stand up and try to defend them. You practice crimes against humanity at the same time that you piously speak to the rest of the world of human rights!

America, when will you live up to your own principles?

chapter 12

First beginning in the mid-1950s, a new generation of Indian men and women began protesting violations by the state and federal governments with a renewed resolve and militance. And since those early days, we have actively refused to accept our continued victimhood. In the late 1960s, we discovered an old law that said Indians have first right to "surplus" land abandoned by the federal government.

So we decided to test that law—to test whether *any* law was true when it came to Indians. In California in November 1969, Indians occupied Alcatraz Island, site of the notorious federal prison abandoned in 1963. Our Alcatraz occupiers declared our intention to turn the island into a Native peoples cultural center—the first building to be seen by visitors coming through the Golden Gate; that, at least, would symbolize whom all this vast and wonderful land had been stolen from. A few months later, in 1970, some of us occupied abandoned Fort Lawton outside of Seattle as well; I was personally involved in that (eventually, I'm proud to

say, Fort Lawton *did* become a Native cultural center).
All of these actions were carried out peacefully. We
didn't ask for violence. Not one of us wanted to lose
our freedom and spend the rest of our lives in prison.
We were simply invoking one of the United States'
own laws.

But the opposition, not surprisingly, didn't see it
our way, especially given the hate-mongering of the
times. We were called "thugs" and "Commies" and
"invaders." Men, women, and even children were
beaten—and much worse—when Indians were arrested during the fishing-rights protests. At Fort Lawton
the government confronted us with machine guns and
flamethrowers. When we were arrested, the soldiers
fondled the women in front of the men, trying to trick
us into reacting so they could justify killing us. Those
of us singled out as leaders were beaten in our military
jail cells in the army stockade. I refused to leave until
every one of our group of warriors was allowed to leave.
That got me several extra beatings, since white man
loves to separate the bros from each other, get us to rat
on each other, create distrust among us, beat us one
by one while laughing out loud that the others have
already double-crossed us when, of course, they
hadn't. It's an old strategy—divide and conquer, they
call it.

I've learned the best way to be beaten is to relax

as best as you can while clenching your stomach muscles, protect your head and genitals, and think of Sun Dance. Sure, it hurts so bad sometimes you think you're going to die, or at least be crippled for life — and maybe you will — but somehow, thankfully, you survive. We Indians are survivors. That pain only makes me stronger, more determined. That pain is my people's pain, and I'm proud to bear it for them.

The events at Alcatraz and Fort Lawton were inspiring to Indian people. In South Dakota, young warriors — men and women — began to rise up. In the early 1970s, the traditional people of the Oglala Lakota Nation on the Pine Ridge Indian Reservation organized protests against the poverty and horrendous living conditions. Indian people were living in old car bodies and flimsy shacks — dispossessed by the very government sworn to protect them in its own Constitution. The ugliest sort of racism, overt and undisguised, was rampant in towns bordering the reservation, towns where abusing and beating and torturing and even murdering Indians was a winked-at blood sport.

I trace the roots of my own political activism to the rank racism and the brutal poverty I experienced every day as an Indian child growing up on the Turtle Mountain Chippewa and Fort Totten Sioux reservations in North Dakota.

part iii

growing up indian

A strong leader shows mercy.

chapter 13

Like most Indian people, I have several names. In Indian Way, names come to you in the course of your life, not just when you're born. Some come during childhood ceremonies; others are given on special occasions throughout your life. Each name gives you a new sense of yourself and your own possibilities. And each name gives you something to live up to. It points out the direction you're supposed to take in this life. One of my names is Tate Wikuwa, which means "Wind Chases the Sun" in the Dakota language. That name was my great-grandfather's. Another name, bestowed on me by my Native Canadian brethren, is Gwarth-ee-lass, meaning "He Leads the People."

I find special inspiration in both of those names. The first, to me, represents total freedom—a goal even most of those outside prison walls never achieve. When I think that name to myself—Wind Chases the Sun—I feel free in my heart, able to melt through stone walls and steel bars and ride the wind through pure sunlight to the Sky World. No walls or bars or rolls of razor wire can stop me from doing that. And the second name — He Leads the People — to me, represents total commitment, a goal I strive for even within these walls, reaching out as best I can to help my people.

Maybe it seems presumptuous, even absurd — a man like me, in prison for two lifetimes, speaking of leading his people. But, like Nelson Mandela, you never know when you will suddenly and unexpectedly be called upon. He, too, knows what it's like to sit here in prison, year after year, decade after decade. I try to keep myself ready if ever I'm needed. I work at it within these walls, with my fellow inmates, with my supporters around the world, with people of good will everywhere. A strong leader shows mercy. He compromises for the good of all. He listens to every side and never makes hasty decisions that could hurt the people. I'm trying very hard to be the kind of leader I myself could respect.

So, in our way, my names tell me and others who I am. Each of my names should be an inspiration to me. Here at Leavenworth — in fact anywhere in the U.S. prison system — my official name is #89637-132. Not much imagination, or inspiration, *there*.

My Christian name, though I don't consider myself to be a Christian, is Leonard Peltier. The last name's French, from the French fur hunters and voyageurs who came through our country more than a century ago, and I take genuine pride in that holy blood, too. The name is a shortening of Pelletier, but has come to be pronounced, in the American fashion, Pel-teer. My first name was given to me by my grandmother, who said I cried so hard as a baby that I sounded like a "little lion." She named me Leonard, she said, because it sounded like "lion-hearted." I don't know how she figured that out, but years later I looked it up in a dictionary of names and found that Leonard literally means "lion-hearted."

Though my bloodline is predominantly Ojibway and Dakota Sioux, I have also married into, and been adopted in the traditional way by, the Lakota Sioux people. All the Lakota/Dakota/Nakota people — also known as Sioux — are one great nation of nations. We Indians are many nations, but one People. I myself was brought up on both Sioux and Ojibway (Chippewa) reservations in the land known to you as America.

I would like to say with all sincerity — and with no disrespect — that I don't consider myself an American citizen. I am a native of Great Turtle Island. I am of the Ikce Wicasa — the Common People, the Original People. Our sacred land is under occupation, and we are now *all* prisoners, not just me.

Even so, I love being an Indian, for all of its burdens and all of its responsibilities. Being an Indian is my greatest pride. I thank Wakan Tanka, the Great

Mystery, for making me Indian. I love my people. If
you must accuse me of something, accuse me of that —
being an Indian. To that crime — and to that crime
alone — I plead guilty.

My crime's being an Indian.
What's yours?

chapter 14

When you grow up Indian, you quickly learn that the so-called American Dream isn't for you. For you that dream's a nightmare. Ask any Indian kid: you're out just walking across the street of some little off-reservation town and there's this white cop suddenly comes up to you, grabs you by your long hair, pushes you up against a car, frisks you, gives you a couple good jabs in the ribs with his nightstick, then sends you off with a warning sneer: "Watch yourself, Tonto!" He doesn't do that to white kids, just Indians. You can hear him chuckling with delight as you limp off, clutching your bruised ribs. If you talk smart when they hassle you, off to the slammer you go. Keep these Injuns in their place, you know.

Truth is, they actually need us. Who else would they fill up their jails and prisons with in places like the Dakotas and New Mexico if they didn't have Indians? Think of all the cops and judges and guards and lawyers who'd be out of work if they didn't have Indians to oppress! We keep the system going. We help give the American system of injustice the criminals it needs. At least being prison fodder is *some* kind of reason for being. Prison's the only university, the only finishing school many young Indian brothers ever see. Same for blacks and Latinos. So-called Latinos, of course, are what white man calls Indians who live south of the Rio Grande. White man's books will tell you there are only 2.5 million or so of us Indians here in America. But there are more than 200 million of us right here in this Western Hemisphere, in the Americas, and hundreds of millions more indigenous peoples around this Mother Earth. We are the Original People. We are one of the fingers on the hand of humankind. Why is it we are unrepresented in our own lands, and without a seat — or many seats — in the United Nations? Why is it we're allowed to send our delegates only to prisons and to cemeteries?

Oddly enough, oppressed by the same people, we Indians often wind up fighting each other for what few perks are left to us in prison or society at large. "Set'm against each other and let'm fight it out while we rip them off!" That's been white man's strategy for five hundred years, and, hey, it's worked damned well for them! So, when you grow up Indian, you don't have to become a criminal, you already *are* a criminal. You never know innocence.

I was brought up into a world like that. It's a world

most white people never see and will never know. When they do happen to drive by an Indian "rez" while out on vacation to see the four white presidential faces that desecrate the face of the holy mountain they call Mt. Rushmore, they gawk at us. They don't stop and say hello. They don't wave. They don't smile. They gawk. "Look!" the parents tell the kids as they pass by in their shiny car, pointing their finger at us— "There's an *Indian!*"

chapter 15

People drive through a reservation and see half a dozen junk cars in some Indian family's front yard and they shake their heads, saying, "These dirty Indians, how can they live like that? Why don't they get rid of those junkers?"

Maybe these people, so quick to judge, don't understand the higher mathematics of being poor. They don't realize that, when you can't afford to buy or commercially repair a car, it may take six or eight junkers out in the yard to keep one junker going on the road. Those yard junkers take on a special value in Indian eyes: they're the source of that hard-to-come-by and almost sacred commodity in Indian country — transportation. Without wheels out in the empty distances of the rez, you're utterly isolated. When the family's one working car breaks down, one of those yard junkers may provide precisely the part that's needed so that Pop can drive seventy miles to town each day to his menial job and help feed his often-hungry family. To such a family, those junkers out in the yard represent survival.

Besides, there's often some old auntie who sleeps, even lives, in those old wrecks. And, if you open the trunk or the glove compartment, you'll often see lovingly stacked rows of Indian corn and beans, sage, and sweetgrass, arranged in there like fine jewels. There's a poetry in those junkyards. Those old junkers can hold holy things in their rusted innards. Sort of like us Indians. Remember that next time you drive through a rez and see those junkers in the yard. They're holy, too.

chapter 16

I was born on September 12, 1944, in Grand Forks, North Dakota. My father, Leo, was three-fourths Chippewa (Ojibway) and — he always told us — one-fourth French. My mother, Alvina Showers, had a Dakota Sioux mother and a Chippewa father. When I was four my parents separated, then divorced, and my sister Betty Ann and I went to live with my father's parents, Alex and Mary Dubois-Peltier, on the Turtle Mountain Reservation, about four miles north of Belcourt, North Dakota. In Indian Way, the grandparents often bring up the kids; the old knowledge passes down not so much from parent to child as from grandparent to grandchild. That's in part why we honor our Elders. In our way, when you grow old, you *become* an Elder — and that's something to look forward to your whole life. So being raised by my grandparents — "Gramps" and "Gamma" we little kids called them — was one of the truly beautiful things in my life. Gamma taught me the old songs and stories, and even a little medicine. Gramps would take me out hunting, show me how to make things, how to survive all on your own out in the wild.

As a child, I became fluent in *métis* — a French-Indian mixture — as well as English, and I also spoke some Sioux, Ojibway, and French words. Since every language gives you a different view of reality, I soon saw that there were many realities you had to cope with in this life, most of them unpleasant.

At the time, our family used to work in the potato fields, migrating during harvest season from the reservation to the Red River Valley. You picked the spuds by hand, getting only 8 to 10 cents for a bushel. My job when I was small was to run up ahead and shake the spuds loose from the vines so the others could come along and pick them up more quickly. We lived at that time in a small log house, about twenty feet by fifteen feet. No water or electricity. We carried water from a distant spring or well. We cut and hauled wood for heat and cooking. I worked long hours, grew big and strong, and had no particular complaints about life, hard as it was. From my earliest years, living through each day was a matter of survival. That's just the way it was. It seemed natural. It made a survivor of me, that hard life. I've been a survivor ever since.

I was brought up with both Christian religion and Indian traditional religion. My grandmother believed in Indian traditional religion and also was a Catholic.

Everyone knew that if you were Catholic, or at least Christian, you got more government assistance. I attended both kinds of services. Gamma didn't really get the spiritual relief she was seeking out of the Catholic's religion, so she never stopped going to Indian ceremonies. For medical problems she often went to a medicine man. That's how I was introduced to Indian religion. I was also introduced to Catholic religion, but that was something I lost faith in at an early age. I must have been about nine years old. I remember thinking to myself that I could never be a good, believing Catholic; it all seemed so harsh and far removed and devoid of human caring, at least where Indians were concerned. I don't want to criticize Catholics; that's just the way a child saw it. Maybe they were a lot harsher in my time than today. I understand there have been changes over the years, I don't know. For the sake of Indian children still in parochial care, I hope so.

In any case, I always felt more at home, more at ease, with Indian religion; it made me feel like I belonged, like I was wanted *as* an Indian, and it also seemed loving and caring and wonderfully mystical and bound to our Mother the Earth and our Grandfather the Sky and to Wakan Tanka, the Great Mystery. And, in the sweat lodge and the Sun Dance, it taught you to deal with pain—something white man would always see that you as an Indian would have plenty of

73

in this life. Our Elders spoke of the Original Instructions given to us by Wakan Tanka, and how the very
first Instruction of all is to *survive!* Those same Elders
taught us that we're not here to *preserve* our tradition,
but to *live* it. Those lessons of the Elders have held me
in good stead throughout my life. I've needed them
often, and will no doubt continue needing them.

chapter 17

Around 1950, during particularly hard times on the rez, my grandfather took the family out to Montana, hoping to make some money working in the mines or logging camps there. We lived awhile in Butte, where, at age six, I got everyone in trouble by refusing to run away when three white kids started flinging rocks at me. "Go on home, you dirty Indian!" they laughed, using me for what they thought was a defenseless target. I got hit several times before I picked up a small rock, really just a large pebble, and sent it whistling back at them in defense. Damned if it didn't hit one of them smack on the temple. You could see the blood running down his face and he was screaming like he was about to die. I was terrified.

I ran home, hid under the bed, and prayed and prayed that that white boy wouldn't die. "Oh, let him live!" I remember crying. "Let him live!" A while later a big shiny automobile came pulling up in front of our little rented house. Big shiny automobiles always spelled trouble for Indians. A white woman got out.

She was yelling and screaming and carrying on, warning she was going to have me put away in the reformatory and calling Gamma dirty names like "stupid bitch" and "filthy squaw," things like that. When she left she shouted she was going right to the police, have the whole "dirty bunch" of us thrown in jail.

I listened to it all from under the bed, shivering the whole while. When Gamma came in and demanded to know what had happened, I was too scared even to talk. I just held my hand to my mouth. That was one of the few times Gramps ever spanked me; words and a hard look were usually all that was necessary to keep discipline in our family. But that time Gramps really gave it to me with a horse strap. I kept my hand over my mouth the whole spanking so I wouldn't cry, and he really laid into me. Finally I told him what had happened. He shook his head with tears welling up in the wrinkled corners of his eyes, and then he smiled the saddest smile and patted me on the head. He said I wasn't wrong, but that I still shouldn't have done it, throw that stone back at them. I should have thought of the family. Now we'd all have to pack up quick and get right out of there before the law came and made big trouble. "You're not s'posed to rile these white folks, boy," Gramps said. "They'll come back and get you every time. That's just the way they are." We packed up and headed back to North Dakota that very evening. Nobody chided me about it again. In fact, my sister clapped her hands and declared me a hero. "Not a hero," Gramps said, "he's a warrior!" I took tremendous pride in that.

After Gramps died of pneumonia when I was eight, life became really hard for us. My grandmother was left alone. She spoke hardly any English, had almost no income, and was trying to raise three small kids — me, my sister, and our cousin Pauline. I tried stocking the table with my slingshot, coming up with an occasional squirrel or maybe a small bird; mostly Gamma used them to flavor the otherwise vegetarian soup. I never could seem to catch a rabbit with my slingshot, like the big fat ones Gramps had gotten now and then with his single-shot .22 for Gamma's beloved rabbit stew. Given the cold North Dakota winters, hunger became a really big problem for us. We had no bread, no milk, hardly anything else. I thought that gnawing ache in my belly was just the way I was supposed to feel.

One day in the fall of 1953, a big black government car came and took us kids away to the Bureau of Indian Affairs boarding school in Wahpeton, North Dakota. I remember Gamma weeping in the doorway as she watched them take us off. We had no suitcases, just bundles. First thing after we got there, they cut off our long hair, stripped us naked, then doused us with powdered DDT. I thought I was going to die. That place, I can tell you, was very, very strict. It was more like a reformatory than a school. You were whacked on the butt with a yardstick for the smallest infraction, even if you so much as looked someone in the eye. That was considered insubordination, trying to relate to another person as a human being.

I consider my years at Wahpeton my first imprisonment, and it was for the same crime as all the others: being an Indian. We had to speak English. We were beaten if we were caught speaking our own language. Still, we did. We'd sneak behind the buildings, the way kids today sneak out to smoke behind the school, and we'd talk Indian to each other. I guess that's where I first became a "hardened criminal," as the FBI calls me. And you could say that the first infraction in my criminal career was speaking my own language. There's an act of violence for you!

chapter 18

After graduating from Wahpeton in 1957, I went to Flandreau, down in South Dakota, where I finished ninth grade. Then I went back home to Turtle Mountain Reservation, where my father had returned to live. I guess I was growing up to be a pretty normal teenager. I wanted a car, and built one out of spare parts. I got so good at it that later on, in Seattle, I would get into the body-and-fender shop business.

Living on the rez as a young teen, I attended lots of powwows and religious ceremonies, but I also went to the largely white school dances and listened to a lot of rock radio: Elvis, the Everly Brothers, Buddy Holly were some of my favorites. I was drawn to both cultures. I found myself spread-eagled between them, really, and, like many of my Indian brothers and sisters, I was nearly torn apart by the contradictions and conflicts between the two that I both saw in the outside world and felt within myself.

This was during the last years of the Eisenhower administration, when a resolution was passed by Con-

gress and signed by President Eisenhower to "terminate" all Indian reservations and to "relocate" us off
our lands and into the cities. Those suddenly became
the most important, the most feared, words in our vo-
cabulary: "termination" and "relocation." I can think
of few words more sinister in the English language, at
least to Indian people. I guess the Jews of Europe must
have felt that way about Nazi words like "final solu-
tion" and "resettlement in the East." To us, those
words were an assault on our very existence as a people, an attempt to eradicate us.

We were given two choices: either relocate or
starve. Later, court decisions would declare this com-
pulsory policy totally illegal, which it was, but that was
no comfort to us at the time. We pleaded with the
government to let us stay on our land and to create
some employment on the reservation, as they had
promised to do, but all that was in vain. The ones we
went to for help, the Bureau of Indian Affairs, were
the last ones, it seemed, with any intention of helping
us. It's no accident that the BIA started off back in the
1800s as part of the Department of War. They're still
waging war on us today.

To implement their inhuman policy, the federal
government in the late 1950s cut off the reservations'
already meager supply of food and commodities—the
pitiful little "payment" they'd promised us in those

treaties to recompense us for all the vast and holy continent they'd stolen. Hunger was the only thing we had plenty of; yeah, there was plenty of that to go around, enough for everybody. When frantic mothers took their bloated-bellied children to the clinic, the nurses smiled and told them the children just had "gas." A little girl who lived right near us on the reservation died of malnutrition. Sounds like "termination" to me.

"Termination" was nothing new in red-white relations, really. They'd been trying to terminate us since 1492. They've always wanted to get rid of us, and I suppose they'll never stop trying. Indian people were offered money to get off the rez and move to cities like Minneapolis, Milwaukee, Cleveland, Los Angeles, and Chicago, where all those wonderful inner-city slums and mean streets were waiting for us. With the reservation under threat of termination, housing was severely limited. Our lands were being leased right out from under us by white ranchers and mining interests, or annexed by the U.S. government. My family, like many others, wound up with nowhere to stay. We were being all but forced off the rez to go to the newly sprouting urban "red ghettos" the government was so keen on sending us to. Sometimes we shuttled between relatives, sometimes we slept in the car.

. . .

I was about fourteen at the time. My dad, who'd returned to live with us, had started attending community meetings on the reservation to discuss the
government's decision to terminate Turtle Mountain.
I went along with him to those meetings, more to eat
the few little snacks they served on such occasions than
to hear the political arguments. But at one of those
meetings I chanced to do a little listening for a change,
and something started stirring deep inside me — even
deeper than the hunger in my belly. Some women
were weeping aloud about having starving children at
home. One Ojibway lady, a cousin of mine — I'll always remember it — stood up angrily and asked in a
loud, emotional, tear-filled voice, "Where are our warriors? Why don't they stand up and fight for their starving people?"

That sent electric vibrations from my scalp all the
way down my spine to the soles of my feet. It was like
a revelation to me — that there was actually something
worthwhile you could *do* with your life, something
more important than living your own selfish little life
day by day. Yes, there was something more important
than your poor miserable self: your *People*. You could
actually stand up and fight for them! Now *that* was
something I had never learned in school or heard
about on the radio. I'd only learned in school and from
society at large that being Indian was something I was

82

supposed to be ashamed of, something I was supposed to cast aside for my own well-being. "Kill the Indian to save the man!" was their official motto! Now here was this woman challenging me to the roots of my being with the notion of the *People*. Yes, the People, the Tiospaye as the Lakota call the extended family, and, by extension, as I would come to see in later years, *all* Indian people, all indigenous people, all human beings of good heart. I vowed right then and there that I would become a warrior and that I'd always work to help my people. It's a vow I've done my best to keep.

About that same time, I renewed my interest in Indian religion and Indian Way, taking part in ceremonies and sensing something echoing deep inside myself. One night in 1958, a few friends and I sneaked out to watch the Sun Dance at Turtle Mountain, which was held secretly because piercing went on, which was illegal at the time. We got a few close-up glimpses of the Sun Dancers, with the rivulets of blood running down their chests. I was impressed that no one was screaming or hollering or whimpering. Those guys looked fiercely proud; I envied them and vowed that someday I would be a Sun Dancer. Then, my friends and I were actually arrested by BIA police as we came out of the Sun Dance grounds. They claimed we were drunk—a total lie—and jailed us overnight. They were afraid to arrest the Sun Dancers, who would surely have put up a fight, but we young teenagers were there, and we were Indian, so why not arrest us? They did. Here I was, not yet fifteen, and already I was getting firsthand experience in government-fabricated criminal charges and false imprisonment. I began to realize that my real crime was simply being who I was — an Indian.

So speaking my language was my first crime, and practicing my religion was the second. When I was also arrested that winter for siphoning some diesel fuel from an army reserve truck to heat my grandmother's freezing house, I was arrested again and spent a couple of weeks in jail. That was my first stretch of hard time. So trying to keep my family from freezing was my third crime, the third strike against me. Henceforth, I would be considered "incorrigible." My career as a "hardened criminal" was already well on its way.

That harvest-time I'd planned to work in the potato fields to earn money for clothes and return to school. But in 1958 there was an early September frost that year, then a blizzard, killing the crops. No work, no money. Winter was coming fast and hard. No way I could go back to school. I had only rags to wear.

I remember, I'd gotten more and more interested in Indian art, especially painting. Even as a little kid I'd once found a pocketknife in the trash, sharpened

it up and started carving pieces of wood—little statu-
ettes of buffalos and dogs and birds, stuff like that. I
learned to draw before I could read or write, and it
was a kind of a way to communicate for me. I was an
A student in school art classes. I was especially impressed by one particular man I met on the Fort Totten
Reservation who went around to people's homes, painting pictures in exchange for his room and board. I was
fascinated by his lifestyle and the way he communi-
cated with people through his art. That, I decided,
would be the most wonderful life, just traveling around
and earning your living as an artist.

Dreamer that I was, I wrote to an art school I'd
heard of in Santa Fe and tried to get a scholarship.
They said no, but try again. I tried again a while later.
Same reply: *no.* I often wonder what my life would
have been like if I'd have just gotten that scholarship.

part iv

becoming political

During the siege at Wounded

Knee more than two hundred

and fifty thousand rounds

were fired at our people by

U.S. marshals, FBI agents,

the tribal police, the

GOONs, and white

vigilantes. These boys weren't

kidding. And neither were we.

chapter 13

In 1959, when I was fifteen, my mother moved to Portland under the government's relocation program. I saved money for bus fare and headed out West to join her. I remember, when I got to Portland, I had exactly ten cents left to my name and a phone number my mom had given me to get in touch with her. I wandered around Portland, fascinated by the tall buildings and the busy waterfront. It could have been on a different planet for all it resembled the rez.

I soon hit out on my own, working for a time in California as a migrant worker before winding up in Seattle, where I worked for a time at a construction job and then became part-owner of an auto-body shop. We used the second floor, above the garage, as a halfway house for Indians in need — and there were always plenty of those. We started doing repair jobs for friends for next to nothing, and before long we got so deep into debt that we had to close the shop. My one attempt at capitalism was over, scuttled by that old Indian weakness: *sharing* with others. It's a practice that means we're rich as a people, but poor as individuals.

I remember one night, while watching television, I caught a segment on the local evening news in which a young Indian woman was screaming and crying, blood running down her face from police batons as she was arrested for taking part in a protest for Native fishing rights. The police were brutal as they arrested these people, who were only trying to protect their traditional rights.

I saw Native children being pushed and knocked around, falling down on bloody knees as they tried to defend their parents' fishing nets and boats. It tore at my heart to hear their shrill, terrified cries as they pleaded desperately with the police to leave their nets and boats, their very livelihood, alone.

As I watched in growing amazement, utterly outraged, I learned that these Native people of the Northwest were simply trying to maintain the rights clearly guaranteed to them under formal and still-binding treaties with the U.S. government. All through this turbulent time I had seen what the government was willing to do to innocent people if they perceived these individuals to somehow be an economic or social threat.

The sportsmen and commercial fishers were complaining. They said that Indians were harvesting too many fish (in actuality, less than one percent of the total harvest!). They demanded it be stopped, regardless of whether or not these Native people had a legal right to fish the lakes and rivers, and regardless of the fact that, in exchange for that legal right and little else, they'd given away virtually the whole of the Pacific Northwest. The TV report showed, by sharp contrast to the Indian fishermen in their little craft, the two-to-three-mile-long nets and huge fishing ships used by the commercial fishermen. To press their rights, local Indian people staged the series of "fish-ins" that had prompted the other side's vicious campaign of government-supported violence against them.

Although I'd been staying away from politics to earn a living, that scene I'd just witnessed on TV was an awakening to me, an electric shock to my dormant Native soul. Even though I was young, I felt I could no longer ignore the Native struggle so long as one Indian was being mistreated. Like so many others who were shaken out of their submission and lethargy and indifference during the 1960s, I joined the fight for civil and human and Indian rights. I decided that wherever I went in America from that day on, I would do everything possible to help my people.

chapter 20

The government for much of the latter half of the twentieth century had tried to get rid of us by dumping us into the multicolored racial refuse heaps of the inner cities, but the unintended result was that relocation created a new current of ideas between the outside world and the isolated reservations. This new underclass of "urban Indians" quickly grew politically savvy, becoming part of the broad spectrum of activist, even militantly activist, movements that were then springing up thoughout the society at large. Instead of reacting defensively to white man's chosen terms like "termination" and "relocation," Indians on and off the rez began talking seriously and passionately about "sovereignty" and "treaty rights," about "reparations" as well as the "return of ancestral lands."

The American Indian Movement (AIM) was born out of this turmoil, first in Minneapolis—founded by Clyde Bellecourt, Dennis Banks, and George Mitchell, all Ojibway, graduates of that Indian finishing school, the Minnesota state penitentiary—then spreading to

other urban centers around the country, and attract-
ing—in fact, creating—a whole new "rogue's gallery"
of Native activists. The attempt to destroy us had only
made us stronger, more aware, more dedicated. Every
single one of us was willing to lay down our life for
our cause, which was the very survival of Indian peoples.

From these roots, my involvement in a continuing
array of AIM-style political groups and activities was
assured. The growth of the Indian movement and the
history of AIM are intertwined with my personal history. In the mid-1960s, I worked in the Northwest with
the Indian fishing rights struggle. In the late '60s, I was
active in the antiwar movement. In 1970, even while
the Alcatraz Island takeover was still going on, we laid
claim to surplus Indian land outside Seattle at Fort
Lawton. We found our inspiration and our strategy in
the example and message of AIM leaders such as Dennis Banks, John Trudell, Russell Means, Eddie
Benton-Banai, and Clyde and Vernon Bellecourt, all
imperfect men, no doubt, yet men whose vision and
bravery and fiery, even incendiary, words gave voice to
a whole generation of Indian activists, myself included.

And so out of seeming death came a new life, a
new vision, a new flowering of Indian Way. Instead of
disappearing, dissolving as a people, as we were expected to do, we found a new social consciousness and

a new sense of ourselves in the human cauldron of the cities. Out from under the Big Brother eye of the BIA on the reservations, we became politically streetwise. This was the time, remember, of the anti–Vietnam War movement and the New Left, of Black Power and Kent State and Watergate, of the Symbionese Liberation Army and the Weathermen. The notion of Red Power was inevitable. We didn't even have to invent a cause. We had one we'd been born with: the very survival of our people as a People.

A new generation of spirit-warriors was being born and raised in the racial morass of America's cities, tough young men and woman with brains and conscience and eloquence and guts they were willing to spill on behalf of this implacable upstart notion: the People. Yes, the People. This wasn't Communism. We didn't give a damn about the Communists. This wasn't anti-Americanism. We expected nothing from America except that it live up to its own laws, its own Constitution. This wasn't anti-*any*thing. This was *pro*-Indianism. Something new, an intertwining of traditional Indian Way and spiritual values with urban political savvy and an absolute dedication to our cause. The government finally abandoned its utterly failed termination policy. They saw it wasn't working, and that we were just getting stronger, more "hardened." So the termination policy was stopped. But we knew the government would quickly regroup and look for other ways to destroy us.

94

chapter 21

AIM was a trivial annoyance to the U.S. government in that tumultuous era. Politically, we were nowhere in the national consciousness, much less conscience. America really didn't give a damn about Indians unless we staged takeovers like Alcatraz, Fort Lawton, the BIA building in Washington, D.C., and Wounded Knee. Even then the public was more amused or temporarily outraged than really concerned. Their ignorance and indifference allowed — and continue to allow — a cancer to grow within the American body politic. The federal government — or, to be more accurate, certain elements within it — set out to destroy us in myriad subtle and not-so-subtle ways. They hid behind their usual cloak of "national security" to do their dirty work. Their first tactic: forget the law, the law's for suckers, subvert the law at will to get your man, however innocent he may be; suborn the whole legal and judicial systems; lie whenever and wherever you have to to keep the focus of inquiry on your victims, not on your own crimes.

I have to admit, they succeeded brilliantly. In the name of Law, they violated every law on the books, and, in their deliberate strategy of putting me—and how many other innocents?—away in a cell or a grave, they turned the Constitution of the United States into pulp fiction.

By the late 1960s, we were tired of the government setting the political agenda. We decided to set the agenda on our own. When I say "we," I mean each of us who became involved as individuals, whether urban or reservation Indians, or those, like most of us, who were caught between. There was no overarching formal organization following Robert's Rules of Order; there were only individuals and groups of individuals of like mind working together in a kind of pure democracy, a disorganized but vaguely coherent collectivity of leaders. That's what AIM was and is, not a subversive plot, not a radical mob, but a collectivity of leaders working in loose unison, using material means to accomplish a political and spiritual purpose: our people's survival.

People often ask me what my position is, or was, in AIM—the American Indian Movement. That requires an explanation.

AIM is not an organization. AIM, as its name

clearly says, is a movement. Within that movement organizations come and go. No one person or special group of people runs AIM. Don't confuse AIM with any particular individual or individuals who march under its banner, however worthy or unworthy they may be. AIM is the People. AIM will be there when every one of us living today is gone. AIM will raise new leaders in every generation. Crazy Horse belonged to AIM. Sitting Bull belonged to AIM. They belong to us still, and we belong to them. They're with us right now.

I've heard a lot of criticisms of AIM's often conflicting leaders and spokesmen over the years . . . of men such as Dennis Banks and Leonard Crow Dog and Eddie Benton-Banai and the Means brothers and the Bellecourts and John Trudell and the others. I can tell you, none of them was—or is—perfect, any more than I was or am. But I can also tell you, these were men who stood up for the People when the time came to stand up. They could have walked away, averted their eyes, turned their backs, and taken the easy way out. They didn't. Each of them stood alone against all odds and took the blows that were directed at their People. They accepted the suffering of their people as their own. They lived that suffering. Whatever their imperfections were and are, we should honor these men. They changed the course of history. They gave us the pride and belief in ourselves that we so desperately needed and craved. They made a flesh offering of their very lives on behalf of the People, and they taught the rest of us to do the same. They proved that *we exist!*

But, even more, and with even deeper gratitude, I want to honor here those whose names aren't so well known, those who manned the barricades at Alcatraz and Fort Lawton and Wounded Knee and Oglala and a thousand other places, those who never got into the headlines but whose dedication and bravery and self-lessness are what being Indian is all about, what AIM is all about, what the spirit of Crazy Horse is all about. Each of them, man and woman, child and Elder, stood tall at times of great danger and greater sacrifice, with no expectation of any personal fame or reward. Nor did they ever receive any. They did it for the People, because it had to be done, because there was no one else to do it. For many of them, the only recognition was to have their names scratched into a makeshift headstone. But then, it's not really accurate for me say that I honor them — for it's they who honor me, they who honor us all.

One other point I want to make about AIM: There are no followers in AIM. We are all leaders. We are each an army of one, working for the survival of our people and of the Earth, our Mother. This isn't rhetoric. This is commitment. This is who we are.

chapter 22

In November 1972, we brought our grievances to Washington, D.C., in a mass demonstration for Indian rights. We called that cross-country march and demonstration the "Trail of Broken Treaties." It was our hope and intent to set up a series of wide-ranging meetings with government agencies to discuss a twenty-point spectrum of crucial issues, including an overhaul of the BIA, putting it under Indian control, and also the establishment of a commission to examine treaty violations by the U.S. government. What was to have been a peaceful meeting turned into an impromptu sit-in when government officials, reneging on their promises to see us, had BIA security guards try to oust us from the building. When the security guards started using strong-arm tactics on our women and Elders, the sit-in escalated into a tense confrontation.

We were not about to turn and run. The spirit of Crazy Horse was with us. We seized the BIA building right in the center of downtown Washington, allowed all employees to leave peaceably, and occupied it for five days—much to the outrage of the American public, who were, as usual, totally misinformed as to what had happened, or why. We were portrayed in the press as "thugs" and "hoodlums" and "violent militants." Yes, we "sacked" the BIA building, looking for—and finding in abundance—files that would reveal the government's duplicity in dealing with Indians. We piled up desks and anything else we could find to build barricades against the government's threatened assault. We broke sealed windows so that tear gas couldn't be used to suffocate us and force us out. The police themselves broke most of the lower-floor windows. Sure, some of the younger guys, infuriated by the government's lies and brutal mistreatment, started just breaking things up. We quickly put a stop to that. I remember Clyde Bellecourt announcing that, for every broken window in the BIA building, there were ten thousand hearts the BIA had broken in Indian country. He should have said a hundred thousand, even a million—that would have been nearer the mark.

One old Grandfather, a victim of the BIA throughout his life, took a fire ax, jumped up on the BIA commissioner's big mahogany desk, and split it in two! He laughed and wept ecstatically all the while, singing his death song as he chopped. "There . . . take *that* . . . and *that* . . . and *that!*" he cried between his gasps and his chants, righting an ancient wrong with every blow. It

100

was beautiful. He was Crazy Horse incarnate at that moment.

Outside, the police and SWAT teams were gathered. If they wanted a bloodbath, we were prepared to give them one. We were ready to rain down desks and typewriters and filing cabinets and Molotov cocktails if they stormed the building. Some of the warriors put on their war paint. Every one of us was Crazy Horse. Seeing our resolve, the government itself had second thoughts. Murder four hundred Indians in a massacre a few blocks from the White House only days before the 1972 presidential election? No way. The FBI decided to end this thing for the moment, then hunt us down later one by one, which, indeed, is exactly what they did. That's when my name, as a security chief during the BIA takeover, appeared high on their list of secret targets as an "AIM agitator" and "key extremist." I'd already been arrested during the Fort Lawton takeover. I was permanently marked.

The government finally started negotiating with us, but only to end the occupation of the BIA building, not to resolve our original twenty-point list of grievances. We felt we'd made at least one point—that point being that *we exist!* We'd proven that. The government promised to look into our grievances (they never did) and they also promised not to prosecute us for the BIA takeover (a promise broken like all the others). We didn't believe them anyway. To defuse the situation and end their own embarrassment, they actually provided vehicles and an early-morning police escort out of town plus under-the-table money to pay our return travel expenses. Some of the Elders even received first-class tickets back home! The government thought they were sweeping us once more under the rug.

But this time we were not about to be swept.

chapter 23

After the BIA takeover, I went back to Milwaukee, where I'd moved in 1972 to become employment manager for the local AIM group. I found jobs for Native people in trade unions and worked in an alcohol rehab program. I also became increasingly involved in the spiritual side of AIM, the spiritual basis of the political work we were doing. You really can't separate the two in Indian Way. The political and the spiritual are one and the same. You can't believe one thing and then go out and do another. What you believe and what you do are the same thing. In Indian Way, if you see your people suffering, helping them becomes absolutely necessary. It's not a social act of charity or welfare assistance; it's a spiritual act, a holy deed. In Indian Way, we have our warriors and our peace chiefs; both do holy work. But, even beyond that, on the personal level, every Indian, every one of us, is a warrior *and* a peace chief. We each seek peace, yes, even reconciliation, with the dominant society, but we're also each and every one of us ready and willing to fight to the death for the survival of our people. Each and every Indian, man or woman, child or Elder, is a spirit-warrior.

In Milwaukee, I became involved in a curious and unsettling incident. We had just returned a few weeks before from the BIA takeover in Washington, D.C., and I was out with a couple of bros having a meal at a local eatery. A couple of men at a nearby table started pointing at us, snorting with laughter, and tossing out a whole slew of racial slurs and innuendos. No way of knowing they were plainclothes cops.

When we went to leave, those two guys stood right outside the front door, blocking our way, still pointing and snorting and belly-laughing at us. There was nothing subtle about it. They were baiting us — actually, much more than I could know. I looked the two of them over. I knew we could beat the shit out of them.

"What's so funny?" I asked them. I was mad as hell and ready to get it on, since that's what they obviously wanted. But the instant I said that, before I could get off a single punch, the barrels of two .357 Magnums were pointed right at my head. The two bros split and I reeled back into the restaurant, figuring they might hesitate to shoot me in front of witnesses.

"I give up! I give up!" I yelled out, hands in the air, so everybody could hear and see. They finally an-

104

nounced they were police, manacled me on the spot, dragged me out and tossed me headlong into the back of a paddy wagon they already had waiting outside. They frisked me—found a busted old Baretta I'd just bought off a guy for twenty bucks, hoping to get it fixed. The cops later said I'd pointed that pistol at them and tried to fire at them several times point-blank, but that the gun jammed. That was a lie, of course—the very lie that got me the phony attempted murder charge. As was later proved in court, the pistol—as both they and I well knew—was broken and unusable. I never went for it even for show. I wound up on the steel floor of the paddy wagon, chin on the floor, hands manacled behind me, my head wedged under the seat bench for protection from their blows, trying to shield myself as they beat the hell out of me. I lost track of how many times they punched, kneed, and kicked me. I later learned one of them, poor guy, busted up his hand up so bad he had to take a few days off.

So you see, that's how it's done. Target us, set us up, arrest us, beat the shit out of us, hang a phony rap on us, drag us off to court and jail, impoverish us with legal expenses even if we never did a damn thing. That, we later learned, was what the FBI called "neutralization"— and, let me tell you, so long as you have nothing but contempt for the law and the U.S. Constitution itself, it can be a very effective strategy indeed.

Much later, during the Milwaukee trial, we

learned that one of those cops' girlfriends had listened to him bragging the night before about how he was going to "catch a big one" for the FBI while waving a photograph of me in her face. I could see the continuing setup in the works: phony charges, phony trial, phony conviction. It was all prearranged; all I had to do was play victim for them. I wasn't about to do it.

My people at that very moment were at a crossroads in our history. Every one of us was needed for the confrontation at hand. Even as I sat manacled for five months in a Milwaukee jail on those phony charges, the lid blew off on the Pine Ridge Reservation in South Dakota. The occupation and siege at Wounded Knee had begun on February 27, 1973. I wish I could have been there.

Before the jail bars shut with finality behind me, I jumped pretrial bail—which a few friends had surprisingly managed to get for me in late April—and shortly thereafter I slipped out of town, later becoming a hunted fugitive when I missed my pretrial hearing. I felt no more guilty running from my oppressors than a Jew in Nazi Germany would have felt guilty running from the Gestapo. Like them, I was being targeted for being who I was. Not until 1978, after I had already been convicted and imprisoned on that other set of false charges stemming from the 1975 firefight at Oglala, would I stand trial on those original phony attempted murder charges in Milwaukee. I was found not guilty. Government misconduct had been so overt and clumsy in that case that the jury acquitted.

By that time, of course, I was already three years behind bars on the other phony charges. The first set of phony charges made me a fugitive and got me on the FBI's ten-most-wanted list, and also set me up for the second set of phony charges that put me behind bars for these twenty-three years. The same "hardened criminal" who had dared to speak his own language and practice his own religion as a boy was now, as a young man, being hunted like an animal — really, more maliciously than any animal is ever hunted — because of two crimes he never committed, two crimes that were, in fact, fabricated by his very accusers. My life had abruptly turned into a nightmare, and that nightmare hasn't lifted to this day.

Years later, documents uncovered by my lawyers under the Freedom of Information Act revealed the FBI plot to have local police put AIM's leaders "under close scrutiny . . . arrest them on every possible charge . . ." We were, quite simply, in the FBI's own choice phrase, to be "neutralized." That explains the assault on me by those two cops in Milwaukee. Hey, they were just doing their job: joining in an illegal government conspiracy to frame and imprison — if not outright murder — a whole generation of Native American activists. And that's just what they did.

107

chapter 24

The siege at Wounded Knee was in its very last stages
when I got out on bail. I had every intention of going
there to join my besieged brothers and sisters. My heart
and soul were aching to be there with those people.
The day I got out of jail I joined an AIM demonstration in front of the Federal building in Milwaukee,
then began organizing supplies for the people in
Wounded Knee. We were on the way there with the
supplies when we heard on the radio that the siege was
over. I felt downright guilty at having missed it. I would
gladly have died in there, but now there was no need
for that. My time of sacrifice would come soon
enough.

Wounded Knee ended after the deaths of two of
our AIM occupiers — Frank Clearwater and Buddy
Lamont — by sniper bullets. After the government
promised to hold hearings on the violations of the old
treaties, the traditional chiefs of Pine Ridge decided
enough Indians had died. The Elders, who had asked
AIM to come there in the first place to protect them
from the depredations of the tribal council and its

paramilitary hit squad called GOONs (Guardians of the Oglala Nation), agreed at last to end the occupation.

On May 9—after seventy-one days—the weary but still proud occupiers agreed to come out, submitting to a prearranged arrest. Wounded Knee II was over, though its repercussions continue to this day. It remains the watershed event of modern red-white relations. According to court records, during the siege at Wounded Knee, more than two hundred and fifty thousand rounds were fired at our people by U.S. marshals, FBI agents, the tribal police, the GOONs, and white vigilantes. These boys weren't kidding.

And neither were we.

After my release from the Milwaukee jail, I shuttled between South Dakota and Washington State, keeping active in the struggle. That August of 1973, I attended Sun Dance at Crow Dog's Paradise on Rosebud Reservation, just east of Pine Ridge. There I was finally pierced for the first time—realizing the dream I'd had since that day as a teenager when I'd peeked through the tent flap at the Turtle Mountain Sun Dance. I felt transformed, elevated to a new spiritual plane. Now I had given not just my time and my effort and my dedication to my People's cause; I had given my flesh.

That same month, a formal warrant for my arrest

was issued after I'd failed to show at my scheduled pretrial hearing in Milwaukee. I was now officially a fugitive. But there's many a nook and cranny in Indian country where a skin on the lam can find refuge. We can slip back and forth across the invisible but very real border between the United States and Great Turtle Island. You could say I escaped for those months to Great Turtle Island.

Fugitive or no, I made myself useful to the ongoing struggle. For a time I rejoined the fishing-rights battle of the Nisqually and Puyallup peoples in Washington State. Even though the courts had ruled in our favor on the matter of Indian fishing rights, the sports and commercial fishermen continued to bust up our boats, destroy our nets, and beat up Indian people — all without fear of being arrested. Since the law wouldn't protect us, we did our best to protect ourselves. Then I headed back to South Dakota to serve on security at the funeral of the martyred Pedro Bissonette, the main spokesman for the Lakota traditional chiefs at Pine Ridge, who was killed by BIA police shortly before he was to testify for the defense in the trials growing out of Wounded Knee II.

The following May, I returned to Rosebud for a time to serve as security chief for Crow Dog's revival of the old Ghost Dance ceremony, a visionary renewal that gave us a powerful sense of the spiritual connection and interplay between Wounded Knee I of 1890 and Wounded Knee II of 1973. I felt drawn as a spirit-warrior to every confrontation. In January 1975, I joined in the takeover of an unused abbey in Gresham, Wisconsin, by the Menominee Warrior Society. The following month I joined the eight-day takeover of a manufacturing plant that had been mistreating its Indian employees on the Navajo reservation in Arizona. A delegation of Navajo women came to AIM and told horrendous stories about a group of Navajo protesters, men and women, who had been brutally murdered. It just tore my heart out to hear these women beg for help. Again, we did our best to help them. Yes, I kept busy. Not much grass grows under a fugitive's — or a spirit-warrior's — feet.

chapter 25

After Wounded Knee, life on the Pine Ridge Reservation became even worse than before, turning truly nightmarish. The GOONs increased their terrorist attacks upon traditional Indian people and their supporters. AIM members were being killed, maimed, and wounded: two hundred and sixty casualties have been documented to date. A nine-year-old girl had her eye shot out playing in front of her log home when GOONs drove by and machine-gunned the house. The murder rate proved astronomical for a reservation of barely twenty thousand people. From 1977 to 1978 the General Accounting Office investigated and documented sixty murders of Indians occurring between 1973 and 1975; they eventually stopped counting and the investigation was terminated due to "lack of funds." That terrible era is remembered even today as the "reign of terror."

In March of 1975 alone, seven people were killed by violence, all the deaths unexplained, even though, by that time, the FBI had more than fifty agents swarming over the Pine Ridge Reservation (prior to 1973 they had only two or three agents in the area, if that). Seems like the more FBIs we had around, the more murders we had. The call went out from traditional Oglala Lakota Elders from Pine Ridge, requesting that AIM come to the Oglala Nation and help protect them from these attacks. A number of warriors, myself included, volunteered to go. However, we went with the understanding that we were in no way a military or paramilitary group. We weren't there to attack or kill or intimidate anybody, only to stand between the GOONs and the traditionalists with our bodies, our prayers, and a small supply of defensive arms. We called ourselves a spiritual camp, and that's what we truly were. We were spirit-warriors, not mercenaries. We wanted peace, not conflict. The violence came from the other side, not from us. It was entirely unprovoked and obviously long planned. It also obviously went very wrong.

I can't believe that the FBI intended the deaths of their own agents. Their sorry excuse has been that those two agents blundered and trespassed onto the property that morning simply in order to arrest someone falsely accused of stealing a pair of used cowboy boots. That simply doesn't wash—they didn't even have a warrant for his arrest—nor does it jibe with the fact that scores, even hundreds, of FBI agents, federal marshals, BIA police, and GOONs were all lying in wait in the immediate vicinity. It seems they thought they'd barge in on that phony pretext, draw some show of resistance from our AIM spiritual camp, then pounce on the compound with massive force.

They miscalculated, which proved tragic for all of us. In the midst of that reign of terror which they themselves had orchestrated—with carloads of government-armed and -equipped GOONs shooting up the reservation day after day—we AIM spirit-warriors weren't about to sit quietly and wait to see just who was in those two unidentified cars that came roaring unannounced in a cloud of dust and confusion and flying bullets into our compound that morning. We defended the people we'd come to defend, and we also defended ourselves. We refused to be passive victims.

Someday the true reasons for their ill-conceived assault, what *really* was going on, will come out. The answer or answers, if they haven't already been shredded, may lie in those six thousand-plus FBI documents they admit having withheld to this day, both from us and from the American public, on grounds of "national security." Lately, I understand, they claim those documents have been "lost." Certainly it was no accident that the day before the gunfight at Oglala, the head of the nontraditional tribal government was signing over to the federal government one-eighth of the

114

Pine Ridge Reservation, now known as the Sheep Mountain Bombing Range, reputedly rich in uranium deposits.

Many of us believe that the shoot-out at Oglala was specifically intended as a diversion to conceal that illegal deal, which wasn't revealed to the public for nearly a year. The public furor over the death of the two agents also conveniently scotched a planned congressional investigation of what had happened at Wounded Knee II in 1973 and the subsequent reign of terror on the Pine Ridge Reservation that led to the Oglala firefight on June 26, 1975.

The FBI's later assertion that somehow we decided to ambush its agents is absurd, as they well know. We had women cooking, kids playing outside, all of our belongings, clothing, and personal items left behind. In fact, we now know (again, through the Freedom of Information Act) that one month prior to the firefight at Oglala, the FBI had issued an internal memo concerning "paramilitary law-enforcement operations" on the reservation. They had obviously long been gearing up for such an assault against us. And they just as obviously bungled it terribly, to their own subsequent grief as well as ours.

chapter 26

Since that time, the uranium mining opposed at such high cost in the early 1970s has proceeded insidiously. Lakota people today drink contaminated water and experience a rate of miscarriage and spontaneous abortion seven times the national average. Our sacred Black Hills, according to the master plan, were to have been declared a "national sacrifice area"—ultimately, were the plan to proceed, to be ringed by more than a dozen giant coal-fired plants and twenty-five nuclear reactors. A cat's-cradle grid of power lines was to be flung across the Pine Ridge and Rosebud reservations in order to carry the power eastward. Court challenges to the horrendous environmental impact this nuclear monstrosity would inevitably cause have blessedly slowed the enactment of the plan; so has the drop in uranium prices caused by the end of the Cold War; but when the uranium market starts moving up again, watch out. The energy interests are simply biding their time for the most profitable moment to begin yet again. The death of a people and of a way of life, not

116

to mention the death of the land itself, never enters into the considerations of those who would foist this abomination on the Lakota people—and on the people of America as well. That's why the FBIs would come down on us so hard, because AIM and the traditional Elders were the only ones who stood in their way. Everyone else either didn't know, didn't care, or had sold out.

I have no doubt whatsoever that the real motivation behind both Wounded Knee II and the Oglala firefight, and much of the turmoil throughout Indian Country since the early 1970s, was—and is—the mining companies' desire to muffle AIM and all traditional Indian people, who sought—and still seek—to protect the land, water, and air from their thefts and depredations. In this sad and tragic age we live in, to come to the defense of Mother Earth is to be branded a criminal.

By pulling the necessary strings, these companies managed to stoke the government's fear of "internal enemies" and to co-opt the energies of the FBI and the BIA, federal agencies that are sworn by law to protect us, not exploit and destroy us. I think the FBI actually thought we *were* a danger to the national interest in that paranoid era. If they were really concerned, however, about the "national interest," why hasn't the government investigated the companies that

117

engineered all this turmoil in the first place? The only thing we ever endangered was the profits of the multinational energy consortiums that were looking on our sacred Black Hills as their new private energy fiefdom. And the only ones in their way were a few stubborn-minded "dirty" Indians who kept stupidly insisting that the treaties be honored and that the U.S. Constitution be the law of the land.

I was and remain proud to be one of those "dirty Indians." I've been called that all my life, anyway. I have always stood with the traditional Elders from the reservation hinterlands and the AIMers from the urban red ghettos where we'd been dumped so those corporate thieves could get at the uranium and the gold and the coal. It's no accident that the Bureau of Land Management supervises the BIA, which "supervises" us. That's a mighty handy arrangement for the energy interests. Just butter up a few small-time, low-salaried officials at BLM and the BIA, maybe a few higher-up state and federal legislators as well, and through them the "progressive" tribal council factions, willing puppets of the government, would sell out the People for some quick under-the-table cash anytime. When the traditional Elders objected, they were beaten, shot, burned out of their homes by the GOONs hired by the tribal council. When the Elders called the AIM boys to come help them, sure enough the FBI was called in to Pine Ridge in massive force. They armed

118

the GOONs with the latest military weaponry, and gave tacit approval to the reign of terror that soon swept the rez. And all of this for whose benefit? I've often wondered what the FBI boys got out of all this, except the hatred of Native Americans and the disrespect of their own people. And what must they think of themselves, those who partook of all these manipulations and fabrications, when they look at their face in the mirror each morning? They must shudder at the sight of themselves, avert their eyes from their own gaze in the mirror. So they have to live the lie they created in order to maintain an aura of pride and self-respect. Or perhaps their arrogance builds an impregnable wall of delusion. Their own unwitting complicity in the deaths of their own agents they will *never* admit to. That at least is human. We can't live with the contempt of others. None of us can. To save face is a quintessential human need. I can understand that.

And I can understand how the FBI hallows its own. To them, Coler and Williams are fallen comrades — heroes, tragic victims, and true martyrs. Yes, that I also understand. But we, too, hallow our own. We, too, have our fallen comrades, our heroes, our tragic victims, our true martyrs . . . and we have them in countless numbers. I live with the wail of their voices in my inner ear. I hear them always. I can't forget them. I *refuse* to forget them.

They are victims of the energy wars, as were agents

119

Coler and Williams, as am I. And so are you, my friend, and your children and your children's children. The FBI itself is a victim of the energy wars, having strayed far beyond the bounds of legality and human decency in its misguided eagerness to serve the interests of the multinational invaders in their continuing assault upon the Mother Earth. All these things are acts of war against the Lakota people, against all Indian people, against all indigenous people everywhere, against all humanity. We must continue to oppose these forces of destruction with every fiber of our being, with every breath we take.

120

part v

that day at oglala:
june 26, 1975

When a white man is killed,

even if he brought it on

himself, all Indians are guilty.

Isn't that the way it's always

been?

chapter 27

June 26, 1975, started out as a beautiful early summer day, the air sweet and heavy after an especially violent overnight thunderstorm that all but blew our tents away. The downpour had kept us up late, and I'd slept in our makeshift tent city, as we called it, until after 11:00 A.M. I felt a warming breeze as I lay perspiring on top of my sleeping bag in my tent listening to the women laughing and gossiping outside as they prepared breakfast on the open campfire. I heard one of them say, "Oops, I just dropped my pancake on the ground, it's all muddy," and another answered, "Oh, don't worry about it. Just wipe it off. They'll never know the difference." She meant us menfolk. I laughed quietly with them. They were right, we'd never notice. I could smell the wonderful smell of those pancakes and I was already envisioning the thick syrup I'd soon be trickling over them, followed by several cupfuls of scalding hot black coffee.

But suddenly this beautiful and peaceful morning was cut short by the staccato sound of gunfire. It seemed far off, and at first I dismissed it as someone practicing in the woods. Then I started hearing the screams. My heart nearly leaped out of my chest. Our spiritual camp had abruptly become a war zone. I instantly thought of all the women, children, and old people there at our tent camp, and of our elderly hosts, Harry and Cecilia Jumping Bull, at their house up the hill. This was why they'd called us here — to save their lives. I pulled on my boots, grabbed my shirt and a rifle, and rushed out of the tent. I started running for the house where the Jumping Bulls lived. The heat of the day hit me like a fist, and as I ran, trying to wipe the sweat from my eyes, I dropped my ammo bag. Bullets were zooming from every direction. I could hear them flying past my head, just inches away. No way of telling who was firing at whom. I had to drop onto my belly and crawl.

Keeping to the woods for cover, then hunkering low behind an old cattle fence, I finally made it to the Jumping Bull house and, to my relief, found that Grandma and Grandpa Jumping Bull weren't there. Thankfully, it turned out that they'd left the property at dawn and gone to a steer auction in Nebraska. I ran over to the little shack next door, where I heard children's voices wailing out in fright. Bullets snapped at my heels as I ran, barely missing me — just the way you see it happen in the movies. I realized I was drawing

124

fire to the shack. If I tried to rescue the kids right then, I would only endanger them more. How to get them out of there? I couldn't even tell which direction the shooting was coming from. I called out to the young ones that it was time to be brave, time to be warriors. "Get under the bed! Stay there until we come get you!" I shouted, then I made a beeline out of there to draw the gunfire away from the house and the kids inside it.

I took temporary cover by a stand of trees nearby and tried to figure out what in hell was going on. Two cars, those shiny ones that always meant trouble for Indians, were parked askew from each other in a field out toward the road, maybe a hundred and fifty yards away. That's where the first shots I'd heard had been coming from, but now there was the sound of gunshots coming from all over, behind me, ahead of me, seemingly from every direction. Were we surrounded and about to be slaughtered? I fired off a few shots above their heads, not trying to hit anything or anyone, just to show that we had some kind of defense so they didn't just roll in and slaughter us. A few other brothers were doing the same with the few rifles we had. Like me, they fired their rifles, mostly .22s and .30-30 deer rifles, every so often from a distance at those two unknown and unannounced interlopers who had come roaring onto the Jumping Bull property without warning. We were just trying to buy time, maybe scare them off, at least hold them back for a time. Remember, there was near civil war on the reservation at that time. GOON squads had been terrorizing the reservation for months, with drive-by shootings, beatings, outright murders, burnings of Elders' and AIM supporters' houses going on almost every day. That's precisely why the Lakota Elders had called us in, to defend them against the assaults of the GOONs, who served as the FBI's, the BIA's, and the tribal council's paramilitary hit squad. They were the ones with the latest high-powered military weaponry, not us.

After a while, when we realized that the drivers of the two shiny cars were apparently already dead, slouched besides their vehicles in pools of blood, and that they weren't GOONs but FBI men, we could only look at each other in shocked disbelief. We each knew what that stunned and vacant look in the others' eyes meant. If those agents were dead, we — those of us Indians at the Jumping Bull property that day, whether man, woman, or child — were as good as dead, too. Even if they'd only been injured, we were goners. We knew we wouldn't be taken alive even if we tried to surrender. Only a few minutes before I'd been lazing in my tent, yawning and smiling and stretching, looking forward to a nice plate of hot pancakes smothered in syrup. Now I was a dead man. We were all as good as dead.

I'm telling you here only what I personally saw and experienced and felt at the time, one man's very limited perceptions in a scene of near-total chaos . . . not how it was all described in infinite, gory, and often fabricated detail by the FBI and the government prosecutors afterward. Since you can never believe anything the government says, it's impossible to trust a single piece of their evidence. They have fabricated bullet casings, firing mechanisms, whole rifles, anything to pin this murder on me, even though they themselves later admitted in appeals court in 1985 that they have no idea who killed the two agents. I didn't see their agents die, had no hand in it, would have done anything to stop it had I only known in time, but at that point there was nothing I or anyone else could do about it. It was done.

There were dozens, maybe hundreds, of FBI, local lawmen, GOONs, and white vigilantes out there, suddenly appearing within minutes as if from out of nowhere, and they were all gunning for us. And two of their buddies lay injured, probably dead, in the crossfire zone between us. No, we weren't likely to be gently handled by them if we surrendered. Big Foot's people had surrendered, remember. Even the Elders and women and children would be shot, as they had done with such relish at Wounded Knee I in 1890 on even less provocation. I felt absolutely certain that our own

127

fate would be the same. They would hunt us down through the creek beds and gulleys, every man and woman, every Elder and child, and shoot each one of us as they'd done back then in 1890. After all, their buddies were dead, and we were Indians. When a white man is killed, even if he brought it on himself, all Indians are guilty. Isn't that the way it's always been?

Other residents of the Jumping Bull compound, mostly women and children, were desperately trying to find a safe spot to take cover. I warned everyone that we had to get out of the area, that they would kill us all if we didn't move quickly, and I tried to figure some way, some route, to lead them out and away. It seemed impossible. We needed a miracle. Somewhere in the distance, above the rapid staccato of gunfire, I could hear the drone of a small spotter plane that was circling high above us. I couldn't believe that all of this was happening. I still couldn't believe that our wonderful, peaceful morning could have been shattered by such insane and murderous violence. I didn't know then why we had come under such a vicious attack. I knew only that my job, my personal duty before all else, was to help protect these innocent women and terrified children. I knew I couldn't give in to my own fear, and I worried that someone else's panic could spell all of our deaths.

As documents released twenty years later, in 1995, through the Freedom of Information Act, confirmed, a virtual army—lawmen, GOONs, SWAT teams, vigilantes, BIA police, you name it—had been gathering in the area for a planned paramilitary assault on the Pine Ridge reservation. And now the day had finally come. This raid had obviously been preplanned. Maybe they figured they could come in and finish us off after the two agents had drawn our fire, giving them the excuse they needed. There seemed absolutely no way out of there for us.

And yet, despite being surrounded by hundreds of lawmen, every one of our group was able to make it out of the death zone—except poor, young, frightened Joe Killsright Stuntz, a twenty-one-year-old dedicated AIMster, shot in the forehead by a bullet from an unknown assailant's gun, some say a sniper, some say an assassin. Only his killers would know, and they've never been investigated. Since the government holds—and withholds as it sees fit—all the evidence, it's impossible to be certain what really happened.

Joe had taken up a rear-guard position to defend the rest of us while we began our escape. We gave him the Indian name Killsright at a posthumous ceremony we held for him. I'm glad he got it. I know he takes comfort in it. That's the sacred name he's known by now in the Sky World.

Hey, Killsright, keep the campfire going and the coffee hot till I get there. I won't be long.

That day, in the midst of hundreds of enraged pursuers, a terrified band of a few dozen men, women, children, and Elders were somehow rendered invisible. I credit that to Crow Dog's revival of the Ghost Dance. For that specific occasion, the Creator, Wakan Tanka, loaned each of us an invisible ghost shirt, impervious to white man's bullets. I don't know why Joe Killsright Stuntz didn't get his in time; maybe he was just reaching out his hand for it when he was gunned down. I'd gladly have given him mine if only I'd known. And so the Great Mystery took Joe but led the rest of us out of there that afternoon. Although we could feel the wind of the bullets as they whistled right past our ears, not a one hit its target. There were roadblocks and roving SWAT teams everywhere. How to escape with this terrified little group from the swiftly tightening dragnet of crazed lawmen all around us?

Many of the group were approaching panic, paralyzed by fear, and I remember saying as I led them into a gulley, "A prayer! We need a prayer!" And then we all squatted down on the muddy ground and even though I'm not used to leading others in prayer I heard myself start to pray. I heard my own voice praying out

loud as if from a great distance, saying something like,
"Tunkashila, Grandfather, Great Spirit, we hope you'll
get us out of here alive today. We know you'll show us
how to escape if you want us to go on living. And if
you don't . . . if this is the day you've decided to call
us home to you, we accept that. We don't seem to
belong in this world anyway. So we say hello to you,
Grandfather. Either way, whatever Wakan Tanka
wants to happen will happen. Either we escape or we
go to the Sky World and live with Grandfather. Both
are good! *Ah-Ho!*"

This seemed to give everyone a new hope, a new
strength and courage, and I was beginning to grasp the
real power of prayer. I even felt a new strength, a new
confidence within myself. And just then, after the
prayer, as we tried to figure out which way to run, an
eagle flew into a big tree nearby and screamed that
high-pitched ear-piercing scream they make, like the
sacred eagle-bone whistle used at ceremonies. Then it
flew off, swooping directly over our heads above the
brush-filled ravines where we were hiding. It's as if it
had come to show us the way. I believe it did, and so
did every one of us there. I believe it to this day. We
followed the direction of its flight, and that eagle led
us safely away despite the swarms of searching lawmen
and GOONs. We discovered, directly beneath where
the eagle had led us, a large drainpipe going under the

road. We crawled through it in terrifying darkness on our hands and knees—men, women, and children—finally coming out into a cow pasture well away from the dragnet surrounding the Jumping Bull property. Then we heard shots nearby, and, realizing that they'd they spotted us, we all ran like hell, bullets literally whistling past our ears, and we ran uphill toward the open hill country and pine bluffs nearby, zigging and zagging our way first east, then south, then east again, praying desperately that if we just kept moving we could somehow get away. That the whole group of us—other than Joe Killsright Stuntz—made it out of there alive that day was the real miracle of miracles, still incomprehensible to me. There was no way we could have escaped, and yet we did. I heard later that they had search units combing the area for us, but we never heard more than a distant small plane. That holy eagle did more than show us the direction to go that day. He opened his wings wide and took us under his protection. He rendered us invisible and flew us to safety.

We were, and are, enormously thankful to the many, many people who helped us stay hidden during that terrible and terrifying time at great risk to their own lives, arranging temporary sanctuaries for us night after night. Later, we learned that Indian people from all over had gathered at the police roadblocks and

cheered us on, blaring their car horns when we escaped. Shots were fired at random, confusing our pursuers as to our exact location. Friends we didn't even
know we had put their own lives on the line and spir-
ited us underground, keeping us hidden from the en-
circling dragnet. Night after night we kept moving,
following creek beds, gullies, whatever. We conferred
with our Elders about what we should do, and it was
decided that we would stay hidden in the area until
that year's Sun Dance in early August at Crow Dog's,
where we would personally thank Wakan Tanka, the
Great Spirit, the Great Mystery—who had come to us
that day in the shape of an eagle, miraculously guiding
our escape and saving our lives.

Meanwhile, the FBI and GOONs and BIA police
seemed to go berserk in what's been called the biggest
manhunt in modern U.S. history, a reprisal that terrified the entire population of the Pine Ridge Reservation in a Vietnam-style search-and-destroy operation.
They tore up the homes of traditional Indian people
without search warrants. They threw people around violently, including women and old people, and har-
assed and intimidated anyone believed to be even
remotely an AIM supporter—which, of course, meant
nearly all of the Pine Ridge Reservation's traditionals.

Seeking continual guidance from the Elders, we
hid out with various friends—but one by one most

members of our group were caught and arrested. I finally decided to try to make it across the border to Canada, hoping to find refuge with my Native brethren in the far Northwest, possibly even seek political asylum there. I figured the chance of my getting a fair trial in the U.S., or even staying alive there, was now all but nonexistent. We learned that the FBIs were so infuriated at the death of their two buddies, as well as by our subsequent miraculous escape from their tightening dragnet, that they vented their rage by firing a bullet at close range into nearly all of the Jumping Bulls' family photo portraits hanging on the parlor walls—some in the head, some in the heart.

I've not the slightest doubt that they would have done precisely the same thing to each and every one of us had we not followed the eagle out of there that day.

In escaping to Canada, I was following in the footsteps of none less than the great Sitting Bull, the Hunkpapa Lakota medicine man who, following the Battle of the Little Bighorn on June 25, 1876, had fled across the border with his people after ending General George Armstrong Custer's proud career as a killer of innocent Indian men, women, and children. Oddly, for those interested in numbers, the firefight at the Jumping Bulls' on June 26, 1975, occurred exactly ninety-nine years and a day after the Battle of the Little Big-horn—or the Greasy Grass as we call it.

Sitting Bull knew the white man's vengeance would be swift and merciless. Like me, even if he hadn't personally killed Custer or anyone else, he was still what they'd call today an "aider and abetter." All Indians, after all, are "aiders and abetters" when they stand up to defend their people from slaughter.

Sitting Bull had no illusions about what had happened or what was going to happen. He said:

> *What treaty that the whites have kept has the red man broken? Not one!*
>
> *What treaty that the whites ever made with us red men have they kept? Not one!*
>
> *When I was a boy, the Sioux owned the world. The sun rose and set on our lands. We sent ten thousand horsemen into battle. Where are the warriors today? Who slew them? Where are our lands? Who owns them?*
>
> *What white man can say I ever stole his land or a penny of his money? And yet they say I am a thief.*
>
> *Is it wrong for me to love my own?*
>
> *Is it wicked of me because my skin is red? Because I am a Sioux? Because I was born where my fathers lived? Because I would die for my people and my country?*

135

part vi

a life in hell

The farce of unbridled lies

and flagrant coercion of

witnesses played out there in

a courtroom. . . . This was the

American judicial system at

its very worst. . . .

chapter 28

There were four indictments of Indians issued in late 1975 for the deaths of the two agents. I was one of the four. Only three of us ever went to trial. Charges were eventually dropped due to "insufficient evidence" against the fourth, Jimmy Eagle—whose alleged theft of a pair of cowboy boots had provided the FBI with its fabricated excuse for invading the Jumping Bull property in the first place. Strange, the murders of scores of traditionals on the reservation in previous months they all but totally overlooked, but the alleged theft of a pair of cowboy boots (later dismissed in court) became the immediate subject of a massive FBI investigation.

My AIM brothers, Dino Butler and Bob Robideau, were eventually captured, falsely charged with the murder of the two agents, and then put on trial in Cedar Rapids, Iowa, in July 1976. By then I was under arrest in Canada, fighting extradition back to the U.S. At the Cedar Rapids trial of Butler and Robideau, the jury—appalled at the overwhelming evidence of government complicity in the ongoing terrorism at Pine Ridge as well as at the flagrant FBI misconduct at every stage—found Butler and Robideau not guilty. They ruled that, in firing at the unknown and unannounced invaders at the Jumping Bulls' property that day, Butler and Robideau had acted in self-defense, which, indeed, they had—as had I and many, many others that day.

After the acquittal of Butler and Robideau, I became the last defendant they had left to pin with the phony rap. Charges against Jimmy Eagle were dropped so that, according to FBI documents later revealed, "the full prosecutive weight of the federal government could be directed against Leonard Peltier." The government needed a scapegoat, a conviction to assuage its severely damaged public image. Someone had to pay for the deaths of the two agents, even if the feds didn't know who had done it—as the prosecutors themselves later confessed. They wanted Indian blood, and I became the scapegoat, the one they'd been setting up all along. I suppose they figured that, if I got off like Butler and Robideau, it would somehow be open season on FBI agents. That may be understandable but it's also absurd, of course—pure fantasy on their part. There was never any open season on FBI agents by Indian people, nor was there ever any plan or even suggestion for one. Maybe some of those FBI agents actually believed the disinformation their own agency was shamelessly handing out for public consumption. But, one thing was for sure, there *had* been an open season for several years on the traditional Indian people of Pine Ridge and on their AIM supporters. Examine the death toll over those years on Pine Ridge if you doubt it. FBI deaths by violence: two, agents Coler and Williams. AIM/traditional deaths by violence: sixty and counting, even by the government's own statistics; we believe the number is much higher. May all their souls, every single one, rest in peace.

I was arrested in western Canada on February 6, 1976, the date from which my sentence officially begins. After hiding out in South Dakota for several weeks, I'd slipped across the Canadian border and had been living with some Native brethren, to whom I'll always be grateful, in the Rocky Mountains of British Columbia. For most of that year I was jailed in Vancouver, fighting extradition to the U.S. The FBI was determined to do anything, however illegal, to get me back, and it did. Fraudulent affidavits from an Indian woman named Myrtle Poor Bear were presented to the Canadian courts, claiming that she was an "eyewitness" to the agents' deaths and also an ex-girlfriend of mine. Furthermore, she claimed that I was the father of her children. If you've ever had someone proclaim a total and utter lie about you—and realized that everyone who heard it believed that lie—you can have some slight understanding of how shocked and sickened I felt that day at the extradition hearing, when I heard read in that Canadian court the lies they'd stuffed in that poor woman's mouth. Poor Bear's statements about me in court made front-page headlines in Vancouver:

"Peltier's Girlfriend Testifies Against Him,
Claiming She Was an Eyewitness."

I had not the slightest idea who this woman was, having never met or even heard of her in my life. She, like me, like each and every one of us, was a pawn in the government's illegal and malicious game. Several years ago, evidence was uncovered that flatly proved the government had suborned this witness and coerced her false affidavits. They knowingly and with despicable cruelty manipulated and terrified a poor and helpless Indian woman into giving false testimony in order to convince the Canadian government to extradite me, another of their victims. Her affadavits have since been exposed for the misstatements they were, and elected Canadian officials have demanded my return to Canada, expressing shock at the U.S. government's willful misrepresentations in gaining my extradition.

chapter 23

Since the day of my capture by the Royal Canadian Mounted Police, my life has become one unending blur of jails and prisons, with occasional visits to courtrooms—first in Canada for my extradition hearings, since then here in the States. Handcuffs and leg-irons and strip searches—"spread'm, Tonto"—have become my daily routine. They don't just take your freedom from you—which you'd think would be enough—but they demean and humiliate you, it seems, whenever and wherever possible. They create vastly more crime and injustice and inhumanity than they ever prevent. All prisons, without exception, are cruel and unusual punishment. Every one of them should be declared unconstitutional.

As a supposed "cop killer," I got special attention from the start. In my first jail in Canada, a special guard was stationed outside my cell throughout the night; that would be the norm over the coming months. When I was brought the next day to the metropolitan jail in Vancouver, I found myself surrounded by a group of openly angry cops. One of them removed my handcuffs—so they could blame what was coming on me, I suppose—and the others rolled up their sleeves and started coming at me with clenched fists, absolute hatred on their faces. I got ready to fight back as best I could—I figured I could lay two or three of them out before they got me—but, I can tell you, for a few minutes I was pretty sure they'd kill me right there. Only the intervention of the RCMP sergeant who'd brought me there saved me that time. Yeah, there *are* good cops, lots of 'em. But there will always be the others, too. You quickly learn within the walls that you're at the mercy of anyone with a sadistic streak; and there's seldom any shortage of those.

I could see out of my little cell window in that first Vancouver jail, and as I pulled myself up on the bars I looked out and saw—of all people—my *mother* standing down there below in the street. I yelled out at her—*"Maaaaa! Maaaaa!"*—but when I looked down there again she was gone. It was like some apparition had appeared to me, but she later told me that it *had* been her, and she'd heard me calling.

That same afternoon I was moved from the metropolitan jail to Oakalla Prison. I was processed and assigned to a high-security cellblock, where some fellow Indian inmates learned who I was and offered to provide me with a security guard of my own. Almost immediately I was moved to an even higher security tier — just one level above death row. All six cells on that level were emptied so I could have the place to myself. My own cell, my seemingly eternal personal world, was five feet by nine feet — pretty typical almost everywhere, I've found — and was furnished with the usual seatless steel commode, sink, and steel bunk with a two-inch mattress, two sheets, one blanket, no pillow; no personal belongings, not even a book to read. The only light came through the front bars. After my legal team began to file motions in court and got representatives from foreign embassies to visit my cell, conditions improved; I was allowed books, art materials, newspapers, and even a TV stationed out in front of my cell on my exercise area, which consisted of a space about twenty-five feet long and fifteen feet wide. I later learned I was getting the exact same treatment as an inmate on death row.

For a while they even put me in a cell on death row itself right between two inmates who were about to be executed — one of them an Indian, the other a white guy who'd been convicted of killing an RCMP officer while robbing a store and was scheduled to be hanged the following morning. I guess they put me there so I could get the feel of it. The gallows was visible a few feet from our cells in another room. They thoughtfully left open the door so we could see the

scaffold with its two hanging ropes. The white guy
didn't say much. He just sat there on his bunk, staring
at the floor, head down, hands clutched tightly between his legs. I noticed that one of his knees kept
shaking uncontrollably. And he made a shrill whistling
sound when he breathed. Amazingly, in a movielike
last reprieve, they came in and informed us the next
morning that the government had just abolished the
death penalty. My two fellow death row inmates were
given life sentences, which meant they had to do a
minimum of twenty-five years. If they lived, they're due
to get out just about now.

A few of the guards at Oakalla seemed to have at
least a certain sympathy with Indian causes and spoke
to me with some respect. And, as usual, there were the
others who tried almost every day to give me incident
reports, threatening to have me tossed in the Hole.
That was a laugh. I'd quickly learned that the Hole
was no worse than where I was being held, in some
ways even better. So I just shrugged and told 'em,
"Okay, well, hell, go on! Gimme a break and send me
to the Hole!" A short while later five prisoners actually
escaped from Oakalla while being held in the Hole,
and that sort of stifled the guards' threats for a while.
Still, they loved to find ways of tormenting me, mostly
with verbal abuse. They would have conversations—
intended to be overheard by me—about how stupid

and filthy Indian people were, about how ugly our women were and how they had such loose morals, about how our children were "defectives" and should be rounded up and shot like stray dogs. Oh, that got a laugh. They were hoping I would blow up, vent a little anger and give them the opportunity to beat the shit out of me or worse. I wouldn't give them the satisfaction. I would never become what they wanted me to be. I would refuse to be their victim. I am not a victim. I am a warrior. I will accept my pain, whether inner or outer, as a warrior does, without whining, without whimpering, as we learn to do in Sun Dance. Sun Dance sends us out into the world hardened against pain the way a charred stick is hardened against fire. That doesn't mean you can't break or kill us, but you're sure going to have to work like hell to do it. So I never responded, except maybe with the look in my eyes, to those racist goads by those guards and others like them. I refused to be as ignorant as they were.

The day before my scheduled extradition back to the States in mid-December 1976, I was again moved to an even higher security cell. This one had four walls of steel bars and it was lined with thick Plexiglas — a steel cage inside a plastic box. I've often wondered who thinks these things up, who designs them, are there courses in college that teach you how to engineer such torture chambers? A guard was stationed right in front of that cell and was ordered never to take his eyes off me, not for an instant, and he didn't—though I swear he must have gone cross-eyed looking at me every time I took a crap or peed. For a while I tried looking back at him the same unflinching way he was looking at me until his face grew red, his nose twitched, and he raised a beefy arm with a trembling clenched fist, his eyes more fearful and pleading than murderous. I half smiled, shrugged, and looked away. We both now knew that I had him just as much as he had me. We were both prisoners, that guard and me.

I guess I was momentarily given some vague optimism by the Canadian Minister of Justice's promise through my attorneys that, once I had signed the extradition papers, I would be treated humanely and be given a fair trial in the States. So I was eager by now to get this over with, to have my trial and be found innocent, same as my AIM brothers Bob Robideau and Dino Butler had done at their Cedar Rapids trial that previous summer. I figured that my case would create so much public exposure of the wrongdoings of the FBI in Indian Country that the U.S. government would be forced to give me a fair trial. I was too naive to see that the Canadian Minister of Justice carried no weight at all in the States, nor had I yet quite come to realize that I was the only one the FBI had on whom to pin the deaths of their agents at Oglala. And, as you know, they always get their man — even if he's not their man.

On the morning I was to leave, the RCMP had a large military helicopter flown into the prison yard. I was given my civilian clothes, and put in double hand-cuffs and leg-irons. I was whisked to a nearby military airport, where I was transferred to a general's private air force jet and in a few hours was landing in Rapid City, South Dakota. Back in the good ol' U.S.A., yeah!

After a few more hours in the county jail, I was taken before a U.S. magistrate to be arraigned. The magistrate tried to appoint me a public defender who looked to me like he'd just walked out of a law school classroom. I told him I would be getting competent lawyers to represent me but he still insisted I accept this public defender. I said I wasn't going to accept this "law student" to represent me on such serious charges, and I demanded to represent myself until my own lawyers could be contacted. He grudgingly agreed, arraigned me over to trial, and set no bond.

I wasn't back in my cell fifteen minutes when I was whisked back out to the Rapid City airport, flown across the state to Sioux Falls, and dumped into some-thing called the "holding center" cellblock at the Sioux Falls State Prison — one of those "finishing schools" where AIM had had its beginnings a decade earlier. So here I was being held in the Hole, without

knowing if I had any attorneys or if my family or supporters even knew where I was, without a penny to buy
stamps or cigarettes or pencil and paper to write on. I
had no way of knowing what was going on in the outside
world or if anyone really gave a damn. All the other prisoners I saw were white. I couldn't have been more
alone, more isolated. I decided to keep my mouth shut
and go to sleep. I had about six or seven Canadian cigarettes left and decided to light one up first, lying on the
bunk and blowing smoke at the ceiling, wishing to myself that each puff of smoke could somehow carry a
prayer up to the Sky World. I could sure have used
some help from up there, at least a small sign that the
Great Spirit still remembered I existed. Then I heard
a husky voice from the cell next to mine: "Hey, man,
is that a cigarette you smokin' there?" He was a white
guy about my age, mighty tough looking.

I said, "Yeah . . . So?" I figured he was going to
give me a hard time about it.

"Well, stop smokin' it right now," he said, "and let
me finish it for you! If you do, I'll give you five postage
stamps!"

Turns out, mine were the only cigarettes in the
Hole. They were worth their weight in gold—or at
least in postage stamps. They were worth even more
than that in friendship. I wasn't about to become a
capitalist and make a big profit on it at this point in

my life. I offered him one full cig for one postage stamp—a fair trade, I thought—"so I can write my family and let them know where the hell I am," I told him. He was very appreciative and must have thanked me ten times as he lit up and sucked in deep on that forbidden tobacco, focusing on it almost prayerfully. I figured the Great Spirit must be answering both his prayer and mine. Strange how a cigarette and a postage stamp can become real treasures, almost miracles, under certain circumstances. I got my stamp, along with some paper, pencil, and an envelope from my new friend.

He asked me my name, and when I told him he got really excited.

"You're *Leonard Peltier?* Oh . . . man . . . *wow!!*"

He shouted down the range, "Hey, we got Leonard Peltier here! You hear me? *Leonard Pel-TEEEEER!!!!*"

I was beginning to realize that I *wasn't* forgotten! But it was almost embarrassing, too.

A chorus of voices yelled out encouragement to me and suddenly my isolation had dissolved. I even heard a few guys call out, "Hang in there, *bro!*" and I knew there were at least a few Indians in there with me. Damn, compared to a few minutes before, I felt right at home! So I passed the rest of the cigarettes on through the bars and they got passed down from one cell to the other, each guy taking a couple of deep drags and passing it on. We all had a collective smoke, and in a way a collective prayer, and somehow those six half-crumpled, half-smashed Canadian cigs seemed to last a dozen or so men for hours, long into the night, until we all went to sleep. Sort of reminds me of the loaves and fishes I used to hear about as a kid in the white church my Gamma took me to. I never believed it back then. But now I'm opened to the idea, having experienced it firsthand with those half dozen Canadian cigs. Sometimes it's the little, ordinary miracles that give you the strength to carry on.

I'd need it to handle what was coming in the following months as I was transferred to and from various jails around the region. Police and guards routinely threatened me with sure death "no matter what happens to you in the courts." I was fed cold, tasteless meals, denied exercise, visits from my family, even showers.

At one jail a trustee told me they had been urinating in my food. When I shoved the food back through the slot in the door they shoved it back in and told me, "Eat this or die, you piece of shit!" Figuring I'd rather die of starvation than eat that, I shoved it back out through the slot. They shoved it back in. When I shoved it back out again, the sheriff and half a dozen guards appeared outside my cell. The door slid open and they all stood there, a wild-eyed mob ready to pounce on their prey. Then they started coming in. I stood in the rear of my cell, facing them, with my back to the wall. "Come on, it's a good day to die!" I barked out at them. "Let's get it on!" I guess that made them blink. I sure wasn't kidding. They all pushed into the cell till it was completely full, then shouted and screamed and spat and waved their fists at me. I shouted and screamed and spat back and waited for them to come. Hell, a quick death at their hands was preferable to a lifetime in prison anytime. I figured I'd take a few of them with me if I could. "Who wants it?" I asked. I hid my own fear. I could feel my bowels go loose inside my belly but I just held it in. Then the sheriff, who had his fist clenched in the air right in front of my nose, and who had been egging them on, locked his eyes on mine, realized he was going to be first and got a sudden scared looked in his eyes and backed off. He ordered everyone out and they all backed out. Amazed, I yelled after them, "Hey, come on back in, you bunch of cowards! Come on!" They locked the door behind them and melted away. After four more days, during which I ate not a bite of their food, that sheriff called the marshal's office to come and get me out of his jail before I died. That would be bad press, so they came and got me.

I can't remember all the other lockups before and

during and after my trial in Fargo. By now my attorney, Bruce Ellison, threatened a lawsuit unless I was given at least minimal privileges, and, after months of isolation, I was finally allowed a brief behind-the-glass, over-the-phone visit from my family.

Finally, about two days before my sentencing in Fargo, I was able to get a rare good shower and a clean shave, was given a set of fresh clean clothes, and was briefly treated—almost—like a human being.

Welcome to Leavenworth

On June 1, 1977, at 9:00 A.M., I received my two life sentences in the Fargo courtroom, then was immediately whisked out the door under heavy guard to the Fargo airport. A couple of hours later I landed at the Kansas International Airport and was driven by car to the U.S. Penitentiary at Leavenworth, Kansas—less than an hour's drive away.

A cold chill ran up the back of my neck when we drove past the long, long eighteen-foot-high wall and then up the front entranceway of Leavenworth. The overwhelming size of the place is frightening, made even more bizarre by its silver-painted central dome, mockingly reminiscent of the Capitol Building in Washington, D.C.—along with its phalanxes of stone walls and cyclone fences and coils of razor wire, and its empty-eyed stone lions guarding the front steps beneath a looming gun tower—all of it seemingly the work of some demented and sadistic architect, every detail arranged, no doubt, for the sheer nauseating terror of it.

I walked in my shackles and leg-irons up the front steps to the first of a seemingly endless series of steel doors. I thought I could hear distant screams coming from somewhere within the building. Or maybe it was just the wind howling in the razor wire atop the walls. Suddenly your mind begins to play tricks on you and it's as if you hear your spirit telling you to run, to not go in there, and then the fear rushes on you almost unbearably, your knees grow weak, you feel as if you're going to wet your pants, you feel like crying, calling out for help. I had a barely resistible urge to turn to the marshals and plead with them, beg them not to take me in that place. I'm sure, if I had, my voice would have cracked and I would have broken down in tears. And maybe I would have done that—except that something saved me. Because when I turned to one of the marshals who was leading me up the stairs, hoping to find some glint of human warmth in his eyes, I saw, instead, not a face at all, but a mask of absolute hatred and a look in his eyes so vile that it can't even be described. He saw my terror and my weakness and he was enjoying it like a fine wine. I couldn't say anything. He just smiled a devil's smile and said in an almost cheerful voice, "You're dead, you fucking Indian bastard, you'll never get out of this building alive. We'll see to that. We'll get you one way or another. Why don't you make a run for it, you chickenshit punk? Go on! Make a hero out of me. Hey, I'll get a promotion if I wax you!"

I swear, I saw his face and head turn into a serpent's, spitting its venom at me. My mind was spinning and racing. My knees wobbled, I felt faint, breathless, and I could hardly take the next step up the stairs. Then that look of utter evil on his viper face suddenly — I can't explain how — gave me a hot, surging strength. The more he glared his hatred at me, the stronger I became. That's something you learn about that kind of hatred — it gives you the strength to overcome it. Spirits inside shouted at me to stay strong, to fight back this rage and this fear running so madly through my mind, to bring myself under control before I lost all self-respect and became the quivering and whimpering victim he wanted me to be. My strength and courage suddenly came roaring back inside me like a hot volcanic tidal wave. My legs stopped wobbling. My breath came back. My mind flashed with bright images of Sun Dance, of the holy Tree of Life connecting me to the world, of the skewers being threaded into my flesh and the thongs being pulled tight until the straining flesh broke, freeing me, and I immediately connected with that holy pain and found in it an inexhaustible source of strength. Yes, this was all simply an extension of my Sun Dance. This was my offering to Tunkashila, the Great Mystery—my flesh, my life, my very existence. They could entomb my body, but my spirit they could never touch.

I turned to this snake in human form, suddenly as calm as I'd ever been in my life, and just as he was telling me for the last time, "Run, you fucking bastard," I smiled back at him and told him quietly, "Okay, let's go for it. But be a man about it. Give me a chance by taking off one of these leg-irons so I can at least make a run for it. Come on . . . then you can be the hero you always wanted to be. Don't miss your opportunity! I'm ready! Let's do it!"

His face turned to a look of pure shock and disbelief. He just stood there, eyes wide, staring back at me in alarm and—yes—in fear! The second marshal, right next to him, pushed me ahead up the stairs, barking, "Keep moving, punk!" I snorted out an appropriate obscenity and kept moving. What's more, I kept feeling stronger every second. No way they were going to destroy me.

When we got inside the building, and I'd been pushed through a series of sliding doors with dark-glass windows, I was told where to stand in one room. While standing there I could see the reflection in the dark glass of the two marshals talking to the guard in the control room through a speaking hole cut in the glass. Then came a voice over the speakerphone. "Press your nose against the wall. Go on, punk, press it right into the wall there. Go on!" I just stood there. Again came the voice: "Press your goddamn nose into the wall or you're going to get your ass kicked good!" Again I paid no attention. I've found in general that no response at all is the best response to the countless empty—and not-so-empty—threats you get within these walls. Be ready, keep loose, stay expectant—and do nothing. Outlast the bastards. It doesn't always work, but it usually does.

And so the long, long blur of my prison life began. I won't bore you with the endless transfers from Leavenworth to other federal prisons, then back again, then out again and back yet again—Terre Haute, Marion, Springfield, and so on, each of them with infinite large and small horror stories of their own. When you're a houseguest in hell, you learn the devil has many mansions, and you keep shuttling between them for no known reason. At least in hell you always get a room, or part of one. There aren't any homeless people in hell. Guess it beats certain other places in that regard.

chapter 30

Some very curious things went on after my illegal extradition from Canada. Without explanation, my trial, which began in March 1977, was shifted from Cedar Rapids, Iowa, where it was to have been held before the same judge who had presided over Butler's and Robideau's acquittal, to an openly hostile court in Fargo, North Dakota. The evidence of government misconduct and willful illegality that had so swayed the Cedar Rapids jury was not allowed in the North Dakota courtroom. Nor was the whole history of government-initiated turmoil at Pine Ridge in recent years. What's more, I was amazingly prohibited by the judge from pleading self-defense, as Butler and Robideau had done on the same charges. My entire conviction was based on circumstantial evidence, most of it entirely fabricated, including the so-called murder weapon that was never mine and that had nothing to do with the events at Oglala, as the FBI well knew, since they had fabricated the entire thing, literally lock, stock, and barrel — as their own records later showed.

The farce of unbridled lies and flagrant coercion of witnesses played out there in that courtroom.

Meanwhile, to be certain the jury was thoroughly intimidated, the government concocted a cock-and-bull story, quickly spread as gospel by the press, that AIM was going to assault the courtroom at any instant. Officials went so far as to cover the courtroom windows. Federal marshals lurked everywhere, armed to the teeth, eyeing every shadow for nonexistent AIM guerrillas. The jury was moved around under heavy guard by SWAT teams. The windows of their bus were taped or painted over. The whole trial was utterly absurd, a travesty, a patent fabrication like so much else. Meanwhile, the prosecution, without a qualm, tossed in endless lies and fabricated evidence and phony witnesses, and the judge allowed all of it. This was the American judicial system at its very worst, scoffing at— even spitting on—the very principles of truth and fairness and justice on which it is supposedly founded.

The understandably terrified all-white jury, eager to get out of there as quickly as possible, took barely six hours to come to a guilty verdict on two counts of first-degree murder. Even though they were manipulated and intimidated, they might have seen through what was happening and opposed it, as the jurors in Cedar Rapids had done. They, after all, were the ones appointed by society to prevent precisely these kinds of abuses. These jurors, so often laughed at and abused, are the very safeguards of the *whole* American legal system and hence of American democracy itself. They had it in their power—indeed, it was their duty—not only to free an innocent man but to set all this government illegality on its ear.

At the end of the Fargo trial, the prosecutor pointed at me and told the trembling jury in a thundering voice that *"this* man . . . *this* man seated here before you" had cold-bloodedly killed those already injured agents at point-blank range with a high-powered rifle. . . . And yet, years later at one of my many appeals hearings, this very same prosecutor admitted in court that the government had no idea at all who killed those agents. He stated for the record: "We did not have any direct evidence that one individual as opposed to another pulled the trigger."

The 8th Circuit Court of Appeals, at my 1986 hearing for a new trial, acknowledged that there had been fabrication of evidence, withholding of exculpatory evidence, coercion of witnesses, as well as improper conduct by the FBI. Why, then, wasn't I instantly released from prison as an innocent man, which I was and had been proven to be even by their own numerous admissions? Simply because, as I've always stated, *any* Indian would do to pay for the deaths of their agents — preferably an AIMster from "outside" who could be accused of stirring up trouble on the rez. That, apparently, was why "outsiders" Butler and Robideau and myself had all been targeted out of a potential group of thirty or more people at the Jumping Bulls' that day, and it also probably explains why charges against Jimmy Eagle, a local man, were dropped. As it turned out, I was to be their boy. Yes, I, Leonard Peltier, was the one. They were taking no chances this time. I was the last Indian left to railroad for the deaths of their two agents. If the feds couldn't get the real killer, they were damn sure going to get me. And they did.

The appeals judge who heard that prosecutor's admission still denied my appeal. Later, in 1992, it was ruled that, even though not one shred of credible evidence remained to prove my guilt, I was still guilty of "aiding and abetting" in the deaths of the agents simply by being at the Jumping Bulls' that day and that I would therefore continue to serve those two consecutive lifetime terms—this, even though the Fargo jury had given me those maximum sentences specifically for supposedly going up and personally murdering those agents at close range with a high-powered weapon, not for the vague crime of "aiding and abetting." Then *that* very judge who had denied my appeal bravely came forward years later and declared that the government had been at least "equally responsible" for the deaths of its own agents, and he actually wrote a

162

letter to President Reagan urging him to commute my sentence. I could wish that that judge and that prosecutor—and so many others, who might have done so *and might still do so*—had come forward to declare the truth as they knew it a few years earlier, before my life was stolen from me. Even so, I'm grateful for their belated admissions.

The fact that I was convicted without any credible evidence of guilt, and that no amount of genuine evidence to the contrary, however overwhelming, seems to be enough to win my release or even a retrial much less parole after nearly a quarter of a century, is precisely why I am often called—no doubt to the great embarrassment of the United States government—a "political prisoner."

I'm told that, at last count, more that 25 million people around this Mother Earth have taken the time out of their own busy lives to sign a petition pleading for my freedom. I'm grateful to every one of those people. I thank each of you personally. I also value the warm support over the years of the late Mother Teresa, as well as of Archbishop Desmond Tutu, the Dalai Lama, and all the other champions of the oppressed and dispossessed around this planet.

Mitakuye Oyasin. Yes, it's true. We *are* all related.

chapter 31

Another very curious thing happened to me a couple of years after my Fargo conviction—in fact, right after the Supreme Court's first refusal to review my case in 1979. One day I was unaccountably and without prior notice transferred from the maximum security prison at Marion, Illinois—one of the real hellholes of this earth, the "new Alcatraz" for "incorrigible prisoners," where I had spent most of my time in isolation—to the comparative low-security prison facility at Lompoc, on the balmy California central coast, near Santa Barbara. Odd. What was going on? Had they suddenly gone softhearted? Or softheaded? Not likely.

I'd been alerted to the assassination plot by the very man who was originally supposed to do the assassinating, a fellow Native American prisoner at Marion—and a tremendously brave human being—named Robert Standing Deer Wilson. Under extreme pressure, he had reluctantly agreed to do their dirty work for them and "get Peltier." In exchange, they'd promised him that they'd have outstanding murder charges against him dropped, and also that they'd see he got desperately needed medical treatment for an extremely painful spinal condition he had that they'd refused to treat for years.

But, after agreeing to their scheme, Standing Deer couldn't bring himself to do it. He came to me and told me the whole scheme. Looking back, I think that's exactly what they wanted him to do—to put me in imminent fear of my life so that I would try to escape. Then I could conveniently be killed while escaping. Standing Deer told me that both of us were to be transferred from Marion, after brief stays in Leavenworth, to the Lompoc facility. He said that prison officials told him he wasn't the only assassin they were sending to get me. They said another Indian, unknown to him but also to be assigned to Lompoc, would have a parallel assignment to his own. Then Standing Deer, having unwittingly played the role they wanted, was kept at Leavenworth while I was sent alone to Lompoc, already knowing—or thinking I knew—that my assassin was in place there, waiting for me. This is precisely what they wanted me to think. Soon after arriving at Lompoc I was even approached by an overly friendly and suspect Native inmate who, I figured, must be the planned assassin.

My days at Lompoc were definitely numbered. Unless I wanted to wake up dead one morning soon, I had no choice but to make a break for it. Of course, they really *wanted* me to try to escape. That would make killing me both convenient and totally justifiable. Still, in retrospect, I deeply regret trying. It was a setup and I fell for it. I'm forever stricken that both of my fellow escapees, who only joined the escape in 1978 in order to help me, have now paid the price — Dallas Thundershield, shot dead from behind as soon as we cut our way out, and Bobby Garcia, found dead two years later in the medical unit of the federal prison at Terre Haute, Indiana. They said he hanged himself. Strange, I'm told he also had an overdose of barbituates in his blood.

As for Standing Deer, after playing his unwitting role, his reward was to be dumped back into an iron hole — the last I heard, back in a Texas prison. They don't kill you just once in here; they kill you every day. And every day we're each reborn, like it or not, to live — and die — again.

Why didn't the prison guards kill me during the escape, too? No doubt they meant to. After we cut ourselves out, I just ran and crawled and burrowed my way through the night over the rough unknown terrain, heading anywhere and nowhere. I could hear their shouts and the wailing sirens. Somehow I got away. Maybe I had temporary loan of another ghost shirt? I hid for five days in gullies and underbrush. It seemed I had become the eternal fugitive.

I was finally discovered by chance in a field by a farmer, who alerted authorities. I guess I could have killed him when he stumbled on me, but I wasn't about to justify all their charges against me. I had an old rifle a friendly skin had slipped to me after my escape, but I've never killed anyone and I never will. He was just an ordinary man, like me. I made a brief run for it but soon saw further flight was pointless since they now knew where to look.

When they spotted me a few miles away, I made no attempt to resist but gave up peacefully. With all the publicity about my escape, it would have been awkward to shoot me there in cold blood. I counted on that.

I was handcuffed and returned for one day to the prison at Lompoc, and then—since I'd only been sent there to facilitate my escape and assassination—I was flown by private charter back to that maximum-security hellhole where the whole assassination plot had started, the federal penitentiary at Marion, Illinois. They had a trial and tacked seven more years onto my two consecutive lifetime sentences. Really, by that time, killing me was no longer necessary—unless it could be done quietly, without publicity or public outcry. They certainly wouldn't want to prompt a real investigation by openly murdering me. I was already one of the living dead anyway.

I credit the concern of my supporters with keeping me alive from that time to this. Their selfless efforts on my behalf give me strength, yes, even inspiration, to continue the struggle. So long as they're watching, keeping out a sharp eye, further plots against me are less likely to be hatched. Though I'm sure the feds regret their failure at Lompoc, killing me would serve no great purpose at this point, so long after the fact. Let's face it—those who put me here think they've won. Killing me now would only force a congressional investigation that could unravel the whole twisted skein of government misdeeds from that day on June 26, 1975, to this day.

168

chapter 32

My infinitely patient lawyers have continued to argue
my innocence in countless post-trial hearings and appeals for the past twenty-three years now. We've had
many, many moments when my release, or at least my
retrial, seemed a certainty—so overwhelming has the
evidence been that I was falsely convicted. A new trial,
at which my attorneys would introduce evidence such
as that proving that the so-called murder weapon was
a fabrication, has been repeatedly denied. The courts
have ruled that the government withheld exculpatory
evidence that could have proved my innocence, and
that the original judge erred in his rulings, preventing
me from making an adequate defense. The U.S. government admits to being directly responsible for my
fraudulent extradition from Canada in 1976. Falsified
affidavits were submitted to Canadian officials. In ad-
dition, I was extradited on a charge of murder, even
though there was no direct evidence against me.

But all appeals have fallen on deaf ears and been
rejected, and each time we've had to begin the lengthy,

agonizing, soul-draining process again. There's probably nothing more tedious or boring than appeals—
unless, of course, you happen to have a personal stake
in them, such as your own life and freedom.

I've already described to you what happened to me
that day. I can only tell you what I personally saw and
did. I shot only in self defense, as did a dozen or more
other defenders that day, and I shot not to kill but to
keep those unknown invaders and whoever else was
shooting at us pinned down while we tried to make
good our escape. I wasn't trying to take lives but to save
lives. I had women, children, Elders in my care. I did
my best to defend them, to help rescue them. And I
did that, not with the help of a gun—for we were out-
gunned a thousand to one—but with a prayer to the
Great Spirit, the Great Mystery, and the guidance of
the holy eagle that was miraculously sent to save us.
Regardless of what has happened to me since, I'm still
grateful that I was given the chance to help save the
lives of a defenseless group of Indian people. That's
the only "aiding and abetting" I did that day.

My legal appeals for a new trial will continue un-
abated, even though the Supreme Court refused to review my case in 1987. So much crucial evidence and
testimony has come forward to support my innocence
and prove government misconduct that I look forward
to my public vindication at an open and honest trial—

170

if the government will ever permit one. Meanwhile, our legal efforts have also been focused on seeking parole and/or presidential clemency. Five years ago, the U.S. Parole Commission—despite the fact that their own examiner recommended my parole—rejected my appeal; they reconfirmed that rejection just recently, in May 1998. I'm told I can apply again in the year 2008. So simple an act by the courts as changing my "consecutive" sentences to "concurrent" sentences would give me my freedom and return to me at least a fraction of my life, if only my old age. I pray that one-word change will be made.

My lead attorney, former U.S. Attorney General Ramsey Clark, also submitted, in late 1993, a formal application for executive clemency from President Clinton, meaning not a pardon but a presidential order giving me simple release from prison for "time served." This, apparently, is my last best hope of freedom. The request was turned over for review to the Department of Justice, which, I understand, must make a formal recommendation to the president after reviewing all aspects of my case.

I still await that long-delayed recommendation from the Department of Justice as I write these words nearly five imprisoned years later. I pray hard that it will come soon. I pray that a golden eagle will fly off the flagstaff in the Oval Office and swiftly deliver that

171

long-delayed recommendation from the attorney general's desk to the president's desk. And while the president sits there considering this innocent Indian man's appeal for clemency, I pray that that eagle will stand there on his desk, stare into his eye, and join its cry to the cry of the millions of people around the world who have written to the president, appealing to him for my release.

Just a few nights ago, I dreamed I was standing in the Oval Office with a group of Indians. I'm hopeful that dream will soon become a reality.

Meanwhile, my life drains away.

My defense committee and supporters have been pushing for many years for a congressional hearing on my entire case, and I'm told that there's real hope for this in the near future. Scores of U.S. congressmen and senators have given me their open support. But even a congressional hearing—no matter how revealing—will not in and of itself set me free. Only people of goodwill in the U.S. government, and in particular the president himself, can do that. I await their—and *your*—consideration and compassion.

I am an Indian man. My simple request is to live like one.

chapter 33

Right now, as I write this in the early fall of 1998, I'm out of the "Shoe"—that's the SHU, or Special Handling Unit, Leavenworth's official name for the Hole. You get tossed down there, into a small cage constructed inside a larger cage, for what you do and for what you don't do, so you can't avoid it entirely. I'm not looking to make trouble. Even here in Leavenworth—*especially* here in Leavenworth—I'm trying to build harmony, to make even this a better world. Stirring up trouble is the last thing I want. That would be the easy way, and the stupid way. Trouble enough will come for sure even when you don't stir it. When there was a riot here a while back, I desperately did what I could to keep our Indian bros out of it, gathering as many of us as I could find into a group, keeping all of us low and out of the fray, praying together much like we did that day when the eagle appeared to save us at Oglala.

A lot of private grudges tend to get paid off in here during times of sudden disorder. The shanks—the homemade knives—come out from hiding, and you want to keep your eye out real sharp to be sure one of them doesn't find its way into your gut, just below the breastbone, spilling your intestines on the tile floor. That makes a nasty mess. I've seen it happen.

We Indians kept together that time and we avoided the worst. No eagle came, but we survived.

Doing my best to keep my brothers safe and out of harm's way bought me a long stay in the Shoe, of course. Hey, listen, I'm used to paying for crimes I didn't commit. I can tell you, I don't like being in the Shoe one bit. You spend twenty-three hours a day in a small cage inside a larger cage. For exercise you're allowed into the larger enclosing cage for one hour a day. Its whole intent is to break you. I'll avoid it if I can. But they'll never break me in there. Not a chance.

Down in the Hole, I dream. I feel myself falling, falling. Sort of like Alice down the rabbit hole, only it's a fall that never ends. There's no floor, no bottom, no stopping point. It's not space I'm falling through, or even time. It's the hole in my own self. I'm falling through the empty space where my life is supposed to be. I've been falling that way, in free fall from nowhere to nowhere, for nearly a quarter of a century now.

Maybe that's why they call it the Hole. It's the Hole inside of myself that I can never get out of.

While I fall, I let myself dream. Am I dreaming or am I being dreamed? Sometimes I'm not sure. Anyway, here's one of my dreams that I've written down. I've had it in various forms many times. Often it comes to me in that state between waking and sleeping. My grandmother told me that was the holiest time, that little moment between waking and sleeping, that little luminous crack between this world and that other, greater reality that contains this little reality we call our lives. The dream always begins back at my childhood home, my grandparents' little house in the woods at Turtle Mountain, back in North Dakota, right near the Canadian border. I'm not quite sure what it all means. Every time I dream it, it changes. And it changes even more each time I try to write it down.

Anyway, let me redream it here, for what it's worth. I think of it as a kind of vision, a haunting and puzzling message that I still can't quite decipher. I hope some-day I will. Here's how it goes . . . for the moment, at least, before it changes again:

The Last Battle
A Story in the Form of a Vision

I find myself looking silently through the broken, cobwebbed window of the wooden shack that was my home as a child in North Dakota. It's as if I've been standing here silently for hours, for days, for years, just looking in through this broken window and seeing all the memories come and go, dim shadows barely visible inside the house . . . Gamma and Gramps, my mother and father, my sisters, all the people who once made up my life . . . many of them only phantoms now, like myself.

It seems like I've spent centuries just standing here in an almost disembodied state, looking in through this window.

Now I hear the sound of someone crying . . . a child. It's a moaning cry, like a distant wind on the prairie. A wail of pain, of terror. My heart tightens in my chest. I know that voice. Now the voice stops. Now it starts again. Now, again, finally it stops. Cold silence falls around me, within me.

Of course, the voice is mine, my own voice as a child calling out to me. My lips are frozen. I can't call back, even though I try. I can't answer, I can only listen as that voice fades and returns, fades and returns, like a lonely, faraway prairie wind.

I've come home, but there's no home to come home to. There's only that window, filled with jagged glass and cobwebs. I manage to pull myself away. My body feels enormously heavy. My feet seem made out of concrete. Each step is an agony. Haunted by emptiness, by memories that refuse to be remembered, I literally pull myself out of my body, which remains standing there at the window even while my real self, my spirit self, wrenches entirely free and flies upward like a swirl of sparks.

Now I find myself on a spirit-walk into this ancient, once-familiar homeland of mine. My feet tread hidden trails my people once walked, long abandoned now, faded reminders of all that once was and will never be again. Again and again I hear that distant crying in the wind.

I come to a riverbank and see squatting there at the water's edge an old Indian man with long shining silver hair bound tightly in braids that reach down to his hips. He's aimlessly tossing pebbles into the muddy gray water. Dead and dying fish, turtles, tadpoles lie scattered along the river's banks.

I wonder who this silver-haired Elder is, since over the years I've come to know most of the Elders of our people. He's no one I can remember, and yet there's

177

something strangely familiar about him. As if my thoughts have spoken out loud, he suddenly stands up, turning to face me, and peers with ancient squinting eyes into my mine, seeming to probe my innermost being. Now, with the flicker of a smile on his thin colorless lips, he nods as if he's been expecting me. He raises one hand, gesturing for me to come closer. I do.

As I approach, I see dark tears forming in his vacant eyes, streaming down his face and slowly dripping into the water. Coming closer still, I'm shocked to see those tears are tears of blood!

Now he speaks softly, and his ancient voice has that same weeping of the wind in it.

"My son . . . My son . . ." he says in a voice of infinite sadness. And he puts his ghostly blue hand on my shoulder, peering deep into my soul.

He continues: "I'm an old man, weighted down by years and sorrow. I am the original seed of life, handed down to our people by the Great Spirit. Each of these pebbles I throw out is a lost dream of our people, a dream that sinks and is no more, yet leaves a ripple on the water for all time.

"I am the voice of the Elders of old, now that their voices are stilled. Their voices speak in mine.

"I am the voice of a people, a great nation, bound now in eternal bondage. These tears of blood that flow from my eyes are the blood of the people, the tears of the people, the agony of the people, whose bondage continues to this day.

"I'm the voice of Mother Earth herself. And I'm also the voices of those who cry out against her destruction. I am the voice of the Opposition. I am a chorus of millions.

"I speak for those who cannot speak, whose voices have been stilled. Whenever the wind blows or the rain rains or the thunder rumbles, you will hear their voices in my voice. I speak for them.

"And I'm the voice of the Seventh Generation, of those yet to be born, who cry out to us to leave them a world to be born into. Yes, I speak for them, too."

As he speaks, the wind rises and wails around us like a chorus of ghostly voices. He grasps my shoulder in that blue claw of a hand and shakes me gently, gently as you would wake a child from sleep.

"And, Leonard," he says, "know this, too. I am your own voice. I speak to you from within yourself. Let the Elders speak through you. Be a voice for the people. Speak the words I put on your tongue. Send them out to the world. Speak the unspoken so that the deaf may hear. Become a speaker for Earth. Never surrender to silence. . . ."

His clawlike hand releases my shoulder, and I watch as he begins to fade, dissolving into the rising river mist.

I reach out to touch him but there's only empty air where he stood just a moment before.

The ghostly chorus of wind-voices subsides with a last lingering wail.

I'm alone again.

On the riverbank where the Old Man stood lies a small pile of pebbles. Lost hopes. Lost dreams. I'm glad he hadn't thrown them all into the water.

I put them in my pocket, and to this day, whenever I take them out and rub them with my fingers, the hopes and dreams of my people come before my inner eye. I think if I could only rub them long and hard enough, that lost world would suddenly come back. Who's to say that other reality isn't as real as this reality we human beings seem so bent on desecrating? I believe it is. I know I will enter that other reality myself one day in the not so distant future, and all my family and friends and fellow spirit-warriors will be there to greet me. I look forward to that.

I continue my spirit-walk. I feel troubled, angry, disturbed, as I journey through the haunted reservation. As I walk, I notice many of the Great Spirit's creatures lying about motionless, others staggering in deformity, quivering with pain. They make no sound. They have no voice. I weep for them and with them. I give them my voice. I cry out to you now in their voice.

As I walk on amidst all that death on every side, I turn my eyes to the sky, searching for the beautiful winged ones who once rode the wind with such grace and vitality. But they, too, are gone. The land, the sky, the water are all dead, lifeless, voiceless. Mother Earth lies barren, voiceless, struck dumb by the mindless violence inflicted on her and on her children, the Indian people.

A dark cloud of black smoke rises within me, a cloud of hatred that chokes me from within. I am choking on my own hate, my own screaming desire for blood vengeance on those who have inflicted these terrible wrongs. My nostrils quiver with anger, with rage.

And now I begin to smell the odor of human flesh burning, a scent so foul that my eyes begin to burn. My heart beats uncontrollably. As the odor of death stings my nostrils, I start to run. Approaching my village, I find only silence where the air was once alive with the laughter of children and the voices of the people. A cold chill runs through me, a terrible loneliness, physically palpable and overwhelming. I feel absolute panic.

I force myself to run toward the first Indian house I see. After entering and stumbling forward a few feet, I freeze. Before me the mutilated bodies of my people — men, women, children — lie strewn on the floor, each in a grotesque pose, eyes open in vacant terror, limbs twisted in their final agony.

I begin to scream, running from house to house in

181

that unholy village. Everywhere the same: twisted, black-ened bodies deformed beyond recognition.

Lost and alone, I walk as if in a trance to the center of the village. Then comes a terrifying and overwhelming explosion. My whole body vibrates. I look up into the sky and see a blinding flash of light.

Unable to look any longer, I fall to my knees, blistered and weak. And there upon the ground I see a pool of blood . . . the Old Man's tears!

chapter 34

I lie here in my bed this Saturday afternoon, my head propped up on the hard little pillow, my chewed pencil stub poised above the yellow legal pad in my lap, and I redream today's *inipi*, or sweat-lodge ceremony, not wanting to let it go. The *inipi* makes each Saturday morning holy here in otherwise unholy Leavenworth. When I return to my cell after that inward journey in the sweat lodge, I try to relive each moment, reimmersing myself in those higher feelings not only for the pure spiritual pleasure of it but also to search among them for anything of special significance, any specific instructions to me from the Great Mystery. Things come to you in the sweat that you don't even realize at the time, that only later—sometimes years later—you suddenly realize were part of your own instructions, what we call Original Instructions.

I was taught by the Elders that there are three kinds of Original Instructions. There's the Original Instructions for all of humankind, sort of like a Ten Commandments that's true for all of us human beings.

Those kinds of instructions come only through the highest individuals, like Moses or Jesus or Muhammad or White Buffalo Calf Woman. Next there's the Original Instructions for each people, each nation, each tribe. Those come through great spirit-warriors like Crazy Horse or Sitting Bull or Geronimo or Gandhi. Then, third, there's the Original Instructions for each one of us as individuals, for the path our own individual spirit is supposed to follow. It's this last kind of Original Instructions that are most likely to come to you during the *inipi* or other sacred ceremonies.

As I sit here, my whole body feels aglow, warm with inner vibrations. In my mind's eye, I relive all the events leading up to and coming after today's *inipi* ceremony. I can't really take you into the central moments of the sweat with me. What happens in there is intensely personal. You never celebrate, or even speak of, the most important things that happen to you, the deepest and most spiritual things. Those are between you and Wakan Tanka and no one else. To put those into words is to freeze them in space and time, and they should never be frozen that way because they're continually unfolding, changing with and adapting to each passing moment. You can only approach such matters with words, not describe or capture them, just as you can never define or capture the Great Mystery itself with words. Words take you only to the threshold of meaning. Meaning itself is something you have to feel, to experience for yourself. So consider this description simply an approach, an attempt to bring you to the threshold of some of the meanings, the higher meanings, as I see them, of what I experience in the sweat.

Many people are terrified of sweats—and not without some reason. It can get so hot in there when they pour the water on the red glowing stones that, if you're not used to it, you literally reach the end of your tether, of your self-control. In that scalding, flesh-poaching steam, you feel there's absolutely nothing you can do but cry out *Mitakuye Oyasin*—"All my relations!"— and be permitted to exit through the sweat-lodge door, which is swung open so you can leave. That option is always available to you. You're never forced to stay in the *inipi*.

And yet, with rare exceptions, you don't do it. You resist the temptation. You suck in your gut and tough it out. You dig your nails into the bare soil of the floor. Sitting there naked in the superheated darkness, your bare knees only inches from the molten rocks in the central pit, you come right up against the cutting edge of your own fear, your own pain. But the fear of pain is much worse than the pain itself. That's what you quickly come to realize. And that's a lesson you'll need to learn if you're going to survive in this world, so you

185

may as well learn it well. And yet, in that fear, when you face it eye to eye, there's an *awareness*. . . .

If nothing else, it begins as an awareness of the fear itself. And then, somehow, you pass right through fear, right through that pain. You enter a realm both within and beyond fear and pain. So long as you feel pain, it means you're thinking of yourself. Only when you stop thinking of yourself can you actually get past that pain and that fear. You've got to forget yourself to find yourself. You yourself are the entryway. Your own mind, suddenly clear of all thoughts, all fear, is the door. And when you open that door and pass through into that other realm . . .

But, no, please forgive me, I have to stop here. Beyond this point it becomes utterly private, incommunicable. To put it into words would destroy it.

I'm permitted to speak or write only of the before and the after, of the simple actions that precede and follow that holiest of moments. Yet each of those simple actions is holy in its own way, too, from the moment at 6:30 when my cell door suddenly lumbers open with a metallic hiss and hum and grind and slam and my Saturday morning, my most sacred time of the week, begins.

I'm already up for half an hour or more — preparing my thoughts, my mind, and my heart, for the *inipi*. I try to keep my thoughts together, not let them wander too

much. I take out my sacred pipe, slowly and methodi-
cally cleaning and polishing the unassembled red
pipestone bowl and the long stem as a kind of contem-
plative spiritual practice. I don't put the two pieces
together until just before the actual ceremony. Putting
the two parts of the pipe together is like putting an
electric plug into a socket — it creates a connection and
releases powers that only a proper ceremony can con-
tain. White Buffalo Calf Woman taught us how to use
the original Pipe many hundreds of years ago. And that
original Pipe she brought us still exists among the Lakota people, guarded over by Chief Arvol Looking
Horse, the nineteenth-generation keeper of the sacred
white buffalo calf Pipe. To us, that original Pipe is as
sacred as the original Cross would be to a Christian.
Arvol has come to visit us here at Leavenworth, giving
us spiritual counsel and an even more personal sense
of connection with that Pipe.

So, just cleaning and polishing my pipe — a de-
scendant of that wonderful original — and sharing some
of its power, helps focus my mind and pushes away all
dark thoughts. I'm proud to have been chosen as a pipe
carrier. That sacred pipe, when I smoke it during ceremony, takes my prayers of thanks right up to the Creator. Wakan Tanka hears us. The Great Spirit listens
to every word of every prayer — yes, even to the prayers
of these castaway children here in Leavenworth.

After rolling my pipe, still in two parts, back into its bundle, I prepare the contents of my medicine bag. Exactly what's in there only I need to know, though there's nothing that would surprise you. The usual stuff for ceremony, but nonetheless sacred and personal to me. I also gather in a separate bundle two bags of noodles I've bought at the prison commissary; they'll go into the pot of boiling water the cook keeps going on the fire outside the sweat lodge. We each bring something like that, if we can — a couple of sausages, a bottle of chili peppers, a six-pack of soda pop, some potato chips, whatever. These are for the communal sharing held after the ceremony.

I'm grateful not to be working my usual eight hours at the furniture factory today, as I do during the week. Though Saturday is the most common visiting day at Leavenworth, I've asked family and friends not to schedule visits in the morning or early afternoon, the hours of the sweat. I also skip breakfast this morning, focusing my whole being on the coming ceremony.

Shortly after 8:00 A.M., the prison chaplain's voice comes over the loudspeakers: "Native American sweat ceremony will be held today," he announces. That's good news. You're never quite sure when you wake up on Saturday morning if the sweat will actually be held. The only reason we don't have a sweat is if there's a lockdown, or a heavy fog, or some especially stormy weather that prevents the guards up in the guntowers from keeping an eye on us down in the yard. Otherwise, we go no matter what the weather is like. We've been out there on below-zero winter days and in pouring rain. Nothing stops us if we can help it. Actually, I love going out in bad weather. It amazes me how we learn to call a rainstorm "bad." There's nothing more beautiful than a storm—something you rarely get to experience in here other than vaguely hearing the thunder shuddering through the thick stone walls as you lie in your cell without even a window to the world outside. There are times I'd give anything just to go out walking in a storm, feeling the wind blow right through me, soaking up the rain and the thunder and the lightning in the flesh, feeling a oneness with the Great Mystery.

Being out in storms was something I always loved as a boy. All that thunder and lightning spoke to me. I used to go out walking in it. They say you can hear Crazy Horse's voice in the thunder if you listen hard. But that, too, has been taken from us in here. Even the thunder and the lightning they take away. Not much they let us have.

Even the *inipi* itself they allow only because of years and years of struggle in the courts, which finally ruled that Native Americans in prison have at least limited religious rights, such as practicing the *inipi* and carrying a pipe and a medicine bundle. Those rights are given—sometimes grudgingly—here in Leavenworth, but at least they're given. State prisons can be worse than federal prisons in that regard. Just recently a Creek-Seminole inmate named Glen Sweet was to be executed at a state prison, not far from here in Missouri. After all his appeals were exhausted and the hour for his execution approached, he asked to have one last *inipi*, one final cleansing in the prison sweat lodge, just before his execution by lethal injection. Not much to ask, you'd think. But, no. His request was refused, and he died without any ceremony. Imagine if he were a Catholic and had been denied last rites! I learned all this from our own spiritual advisor, Henry Wahwassuck, who walked Glen Sweet to the execution chamber and watched him die.

"He was an Indian," Henry told me. "He died brave, like an Indian dies. He'll have his *inipi* ceremony in the Sky World. They can't take it away from him up there!"

Now I wait for the call to go down to the sweat lodge.

One of the bros calls down the corridor, "Hey, weather's clear. Temperature's about twenty out there!"

190

Good. I like it when it's cold. Being in the scalding heat inside of the sweat lodge with all that pure freezing cold on the outside somehow makes the sweat ceremony seem even more intense.

A little after 7:30, I gather my pipe and bundles, head out of my cell down the narrow corridor to the stairwell and make my way down the stairs to the prison chaplain's office door, where we gather around until we get the final OK to have the sweat—or as the hacks (guards) like to call it, the "Pow-Wow." I pass through two metal detectors before I'm finally out through the complex of corridors and outbuildings into the icy open air of the yard. Outside there's one more metal detector check.

With the other bros I stand there for quite a while in front of the locked gate to the tall wire fence they've built around the sweat lodge. Wearing just sweatpants and T-shirt and the like, we're all shivering in the bracing air as we wait for the guard to unlock the gate. But the cold air feels good. And it's pure, unlike the heavy worn-out, breathed-out air in the cellblock. I fill my lungs with the coldness, enjoying every second of it. We stand there exchanging pleasantries, but there's not much joshing around on this sacred occasion. We're all focusing on the inward journey we're about to take. Finally, the chaplain unlocks the gate and we file in, maybe sixteen or eighteen of us.

The guard counts us for the third or fourth time, and says, "Okay, you're in. Back later."

He locks us in and walks away. We may be locked inside a twelve-foot-high steel fence inside a maximum-security prison directly up against the north wall flanked by two towering guntowers, but—suddenly—*we're free!*

Now we each make our preparations. The drum keepers set up the drum outside the lodge. The fire keeper starts the big fire outside the lodge, the fire that will heat all the sacred stones for the ceremony to come. Each of us sets a pinch or two of tobacco, along with our prayers, onto the fire. The cook gets the big pot of water boiling on another fire off to the side. I hand him the two bags of noodles I've brought. Beside him he gathers a growing pile of packaged foodstuffs, a few fresh vegetables, and some soft drinks. We set up the little stone altar and dress it with sage and sweet-grass and other ceremonial items. Those of us who are pipe carriers assemble our pipes for the ceremony ahead, setting them down for the time being at the altar as an offering. We also set out our eagle feathers with a prayer of offering. Then we stand around and chat good-naturedly, maybe sip some hot coffee, all of us feeling good. It's pretty much a social hour until about 10:30 or so, when the loudspeakers ring out, "The count is clear!" meaning everybody's been accounted for at the last head count.

By now it's nearly 11:00 A.M. and we await the arrival from the outside world of our spiritual advisor, Henry, whom I've known since we were kids together at the Wahpeton BIA school. He also had the high honor of spending five years within these walls himself back in the '70s. Henry was one of those brave souls against whom the government built a case at that time — as they did against so many others who had done nothing but defend their people.

Henry's our sweat leader for today. He's a friend to all of us, a wonderfully spiritual guy — and one tough-nosed dude, let me tell you. When it comes to the *inipi*, he sees to it that everything's done just right. Every detail has to be followed just so. Henry himself brought in most of the materials for the building of the sweat lodge — the saplings that create the skeletal structure of the domed lodge, and the rocks — small and large stones of fire-resistant gray-black lava — that we use in the fire. The lodge's covering we've pieced together from torn blankets and miscellaneous pieces of canvas we managed to scrounge up here in Leavenworth. Maybe five feet high and nearly fifteen feet across, it's sort of make-shift looking, I suppose, but to us it's as impressive looking, and certainly as holy, as any cathedral.

Now the singers set up the drum and start beating out a low, steady rhythm. They begin one of the sacred songs, a pipe song, the first of many songs to be sung

193

this day, and we finally start filling our pipes for the ceremony ahead. The big bass boom of the drum catches the attention of the guards up in the gun towers on either side. We can see the shadowed silhouettes of their heads bobbing around up there, staring down at us. I guess they're used to looking down at our strange doings. Must lighten up an otherwise boring Saturday morning for them. I wonder if they get a whiff of the perfumed smoke from the sage and sweetgrass and cleansing cedar. I pray they do.

Now Henry finally arrives—they don't let him in till the last possible moment, it seems—and the chaplain locks him into the sweat compound with us. Henry has a big hearty hello and a handshake and a bear hug for just about everyone. But his smiles quickly turn to seriousness. He checks the place out to make sure everything's ready for the ceremony. When he sees that all is in order down to the last tiny detail, he finally announces: "Everything's in its place. It's time!"

Those are his exact words every time. That's the signal for us to enter the sweat lodge.

By now we've stripped down bare naked, wrapped only in a torn strip of old army blanket—which we've had to use lately since they confiscated our ceremonial towels. We line up outside the door to the *inipi*, carrying our pipes and gourd rattles and our eagle feathers. Someone once asked Henry why we had to be naked,

and he said, "Did you ever see a baby born wearing a
diaper or underpants?" Often the door of the sweat
lodge is compared to the opening into the womb of
Mother Earth. I also like to think of it as a doorway
into yourself and *through* yourself and then right *out*
of yourself. Your *self*'s the first thing you've got to leave
behind when you enter the *inipi*.

We enter through the pulled-back door flap, turning immediately to the left and moving clockwise
around the interior of the lodge, each of us assuming
our places on the bare, well-smoothed dirt floor. Whoever's been chosen that day to pour the water on the
red-hot rocks to create the steam enters first, moving
around the circular lodge and taking his seat beside
Henry, who's already in his place, sitting just to the
right of the still-open door, preparing his ceremonial
paraphernalia. It's still cool inside the lodge; the central firepit in the center is empty. The red-hot stones
will be handed in later by the fire keeper from the fire
outside, each glowing stone brought reverently inside
on deer-antler carriers. The first seven are brought in
one by one—one each for the four sacred directions,
Mother Earth, the People, and Wakan Tanka. More
rocks will be brought in later, depending on how hot
Henry wants it to get. But even before the stones are
brought in, the body heat of some twenty men quickly
warms it up to a cozy temperature in there.

Outside stands the doorkeeper, who will close and

open the door four times, or four "rounds" as we call them, during the two-to-three-hour ceremony.

Next we pray and "offer thought," as Henry calls it, trying to bring our collective minds together as one mind. We pass the sage around the circle; everybody takes a little pinch and chews it or maybe puts it into their hair. And then the eagle feathers are passed around, so we can all share their energy. The flap is still open, and the first seven rocks are brought in on the antlers and placed in the central pit at our knees. We offer cedar on the stones, to cleanse and purify the air, driving out any bad thoughts. Then Henry asks for the water, and a bucket is brought in and placed in the center of the doorway inside the lodge. Cedar is offered onto the glowing stones themselves, hissing sharply as it fills the air with its lovely smell. Then Henry sprinkles the cedar onto the stones, and blesses the water four times.

Now the pourer takes Henry's buffalo-horn scoop, fills it with water, and makes the first pour onto the rocks. By now the door's closed and . . . But, no, that's as far as I can take you here. The rest, Henry tells me, cannot be told. It can be experienced, but not told.

I can only say that four times the door is opened and closed, four times the water is poured from the buffalo horn onto the molten rocks, four times the su-perheated steam explodes and envelops us . . . but, *no*

more! "Don't divulge what happens, none of the specifics that happen to you in there!" Henry insists.

And I honor that. I hope you will, too. Already I've
probably said too much, but Henry will go over this
and see that what should be unspoken remains unspoken. This precaution is for your sake as much as mine.
To speak of what happens to me in the *inipi* would be
like giving *you* the medicine intended for *me*. It would
be pointless, even harmful—to you as well as to me.

Enough said. *Mitakuye Oyasin.*

After the fourth round, and our final prayers, the door
to the *inipi* is opened for the final time and we file
out the way we came in. The twenty-degree air hits me
like a powerful slap, almost knocking me backward.
Yet it feels wonderful. Off to one side there's a jerry-
rigged shower with unheated water that I enjoy shivering under for a few seconds, washing off the sweat
and slapping wildly at myself. It's unbelievably invig-
orating after the scalding-hot sweat bath. My flesh
seems to come alive. I could swear I'm glowing, I feel
so good. I *have* been reborn!

We make a circle outside and light our pipes, and
"offer thought" again. It's all very intimate, very moving. After burning some more sage and sweetgrass, we
empty out our pipes, then dress and have our com-

munal sharing of all the foodstuffs the cook has fixed up. By now everyone's bright-eyed, smiling, laughing, talking a blue streak. There's a really powerful camaraderie. It's a happy and a holy moment. We hate for it to end. But soon the chaplain appears at the gate, and a guard barks, "Time's up. Gotta get ready for four o'clock head count!" That instantly dampens the magic, and moments later we're on our way back through those three metal detectors, back into the cellblock, back into the ordinary world. Back to Leavenworth after seven hours of blessed freedom. And those guards in their gun towers never even realized we'd escaped!

© Jeffry Scott

part vii

a message to humanity

Our work will be unfinished

until not one human being is

hungry or battered, not a

single person is forced to die

in war, not one innocent

languishes imprisoned, and

no one is persecuted for his or

her beliefs.

chapter 35

Out of death comes life. Out of pain comes hope. This I have learned these long years of loss. Loss, but never despair. I have never lost hope or an absolute belief in the rightness of my cause, which is my People's survival.

I don't know how to save the world. I don't have the answers or The Answer. I hold no secret knowledge as to how to fix the mistakes of generations past and present. I only know that without compassion and respect for *all* of Earth's inhabitants, none of us will survive — nor will we deserve to.

The future, our mutual future, the future of all the peoples of humanity, must be founded on respect. Let respect be both the catchword and the watchword of the new millennium we are now all entering together. Just as we want others to respect us, so we need to show respect to others.

We are in this together — the rich, the poor, the red, the white, the black, the brown, and the yellow. We are all one family of humankind. We share responsibility for our Mother the Earth and for all those who live and breathe upon her.

I believe our work will be unfinished until not one human being is hungry or battered, not a single person is forced to die in war, not one innocent languishes imprisoned, and no one is persecuted for his or her beliefs.

I believe in the good in humankind. I believe that the good can prevail, but only with great effort. And that effort is ours, each of ours, yours and mine.

We must be prepared for the danger that will surely come our way. Critics will attack us, try to distance us from each other and mock our sincerity. But if we are strong in our beliefs, we can reverse their assaults and grow even stronger in our commitments to Mother Earth, our struggles, and our future generations of children.

Never cease in the fight for peace, justice, and equality for all people. Be persistent in all that you do and don't allow anyone to sway you from your conscience.

Sitting Bull said, "As individual fingers we can easily be broken, but all together we make a mighty fist."

The struggle is ours to win or lose.

chapter 36

I can tell you this. We don't ask for vengeance, or even want it. I set aside all accusations because I know all too well what it is to be the accused. I set aside all condemnations because I know all too well what it is to be the condemned. We seek not revenge but reconciliation and mutual respect among our peoples. We may be of different nations, but we are still of the same society, and we share the same land. We all want justice, equality, fairness . . . the very principles on which America is founded and by its own Constitution supposedly bestows on all within its borders, even Indians. Is that too much to ask? We don't expect perfection of others, or demand it. It's in our imperfections that we bear our common humanity.

The past can't be changed, that's true. No one can bring the dead back. But we can do something for the living. Economic reparations to Native Americans are absolutely essential for a just future, as is the return of sacred sites and significant pieces of ancestral territory, as well as a fair share of the natural resources on lands taken in violation of treaties. Native Americans, and indigenous peoples everywhere, should be given a special stewardship over the land. They are the guardians of Mother Earth, her representatives, and will always speak out against her destruction.

Such steps must begin with a formal acknowledgment of past abuses. Canada has now made a promising step in that direction with its history-making January 1998 "Statement of Reconciliation" to its Native peoples. The statement reads:

> As a country, we are burdened by past actions that resulted in weakening the identity of aboriginal peoples, suppressing their languages and cultures, and outlawing spiritual practices. . . .
>
> The government of Canada today formally expresses to all aboriginal people in Canada our profound regret for past actions of the federal government which have contributed to these difficult pages in the history of our relationship together.

The Canadian government has also established a Healing Fund of $350 million specifically earmarked to assist victims of physical and mental abuse in the government-run schools that so long tortured Indian children for being who they were. Those inhuman schools, fortunately, were closed in Canada during the

1970s. The Healing Fund should be increased many-fold to assist all the Native peoples of Canada on a continuing basis. Land claims, too, must be seriously addressed. Similar moves by the United States, and by all nations with dispossessed indigenous populations, could go a long way toward the Great Healing that I see taking place at the beginning of the new millennium.

It's impossible, of course, to pay us reparations for a mother or a child or a husband murdered or starved or falsely imprisoned. But I look at our children and I see the future in them, a future filled with freedom and possibility. We Indians were supposed to have vanished long ago. Yet here we are. Every one of our children is a miracle. So let's focus our energies and our love on those children, those holy offspring. Each and every Indian child is Crazy Horse reborn. Ours is the Crazy Horse Spirit. It's who we are. Kill us, but the spirit doesn't die. It's reborn in the next Indian child and the next. So let us bless our children just as their very existence blesses us.

The law I look to for justice for my people is not the white man's law, the unnatural law, the man-given law. The law my people and I look to is the law of the Great Spirit, which never ceases to work, and whose workings are invariably implacable and just. And by that law there will be freedom for my grandchildren

205

and your grandchildren to live in peace and harmony with all other decent human beings of this world. The light I am seeing will ignite, and together we will be able to watch it grow until there is justice for all people everywhere.

We of this generation won't even be here when the world becomes theirs. Let those of us who have muddled our own times so badly come to terms with each other, now and here. Must we pass this hatred and injustice and wickedness on even to future innocent generations? Must we make them guilty, too? Can't we resolve this thing between us now, and finally end it? I am praying that we can. My life is an instrument for that purpose.

Today in South Africa, that longtime stronghold of apartheid and racism, an era of oppression by one people over another has begun fading and a new era of equality and dignity has dawned. President Nelson Mandela, a man only recently in a situation parallel to mine—imprisoned for standing up for his people—now leads not only his own people but an entire state of peoples. He is living proof that the edict of the people outweighs the verdict of the government. His example should be an inspiration and a tool for our own struggle.

Today in South Africa men and women from both sides are being allowed to come forward in public Truth and Reconciliation tribunals to confess their misdeeds and be given political absolution. That, I think, won't be necessary here. Besides, the trials would take centuries. We need not courtrooms but schoolrooms, not jails and prisons but decent homes and jobs for the millions of every color — including many, many white people — who are being denied their human and civil rights every day of every week by the special interests that are trying to steal America. Government must be by, of, and for the people, not by, of, and for the special interests. Read your own Declaration of Independence and Constitution, America. It's all there.

If building more prisons for those of us who are unlike yourselves is to be your strategy, then, I promise you, you cannot build enough prisons to hold us all. I ask America, as one familiar with your darkest side as well as with your shining possibilities, rethink this current craze for building ever more prisons for ever more of those of us born different than you. We don't need more prisons. We need more compassion. That compassion is our own highest possibility.

Democracy means difference, not sameness. Allow us our differences as we allow you yours. We don't conflict with each other; we complement each other.

We need each other. Each of us is responsible for what happens on this earth. We are each absolutely essential, each totally irreplaceable. Each of us is *the* swing vote in the bitter election battle now being waged between our best and our worst possibilities.

How are *you* going to cast your all-important ballot?

Humanity awaits your decision.

We must each be an army of one in the endless struggle between the goodness we are all capable of and the evil that threatens us all from without as well as from within. Yes, we can each be an army of one. One good man or one good woman can change the world, can push back the evil, and their work can be a beacon for millions, for *billions*. Are you that man or woman? If so, may the Great Spirit bless you. If not, *why not*? We must each of us be that person. That will transform the world overnight. That would be a miracle, yes, but a miracle within our power, our healing power.

To heal will require real effort, and a change of heart, from all of us. To heal means that we will begin to look upon one another with respect and tolerance instead of prejudice, distrust, and hatred. We will have to teach our children—as well as ourselves—to love the diversity of humanity. To heal we will have to make a conscious effort to live as the Creator intended, as sisters and brothers, all of one human family, caretakers of this fragile, perishable, and sacred Earth. To heal we will have to come to the realization that we are *all* under a life sentence together . . . and there's no chance for parole.

We can do it. Yes, you and I and all of us together. Now is the time. Now is the only possible time. Let the Great Healing begin.

chapter 37

My grandson, Cyrus, just left a few minutes ago, leaving me filled with an overwhelming love. And yet, for me, that fullness is also an emptiness. For me, life is an empty glass turned upside down—or so it seems when the doors slide shut behind him and he turns to face me with that last sadly smiling look back and waves his hand and blows a kiss to me, his "Gramps." Now he's halfway and more to being a man himself, a real warrior, and I'm proud of him, I can tell you that. We had one of our wonderful occasional visits down in the visitor's room for a few hours this morning. Now, right after today's visit, he's going off to visit his sister, Alexandra, who's staying with friends down in Georgia. Poor kids, they get passed around. They, too, have to pay every day for the crime I never committed.

Still, knowing that Cyrus and Alexandra are out there along with my other wonderful grandchildren—seven in all, at last count—gives me a kind of freedom. I suppose I see myself in Cyrus. And, yet, maybe that's not good. Maybe he'd be better off with less of his jailbird "Gramps" in him than more. But then, damn it, I tell myself, he's better off honoring his own grandfather, his own Elders, as I've honored mine. They're our links not only to the past but to the future . . . and to ourselves as well. I'm an Indian, Cyrus is an Indian, Alexandra is an Indian. We're all links in an endless and unbroken chain. All the grandfathers and all the grandmothers and all the grandchildren . . . we're all one person, one Indian People, going all the way back to the beginning and all the way out to the furthest end of time. One People. One person. Maybe that's why they've tried so often, it seems, to kill us all, down to the last man and woman and child. Because they realized that, unless they did, there'd still be that one person left, that one last survivor to haunt them and put the lie to their deeds, their supposed victory.

Each of us Indians is that one person, that last survivor. We're each the last Indian, just like we're each the first. You can kill us, but we're always still here. We were the first ones here, and when it's time to say a last good-bye to Mother Earth, we'll be the ones to burn tobacco and sage and sweetgrass and say a final prayer and a last *Washté*—"It's good!"—as Wakan Tanka, the Great Mystery, mercifully uncreates the world to end this cycle of time. As our grandfathers and our grandmothers have always told us, we've got a better place to go, a better world that's waiting for us.

So, to you, my friend, before I leave this lesser

211

reality for that greater one, I say, *Washté!* It's good! Thank you for hearing my words. I wish your spirit peace and happiness and fulfillment on its continued journey. Perhaps we'll meet one day, you and I, on the Great Red Road. I pray that we do. *Mitakuye Oyasin!*

we are not separate

We are not separate beings, you and I.
We are different strands of the same Being.

You are me and I am you
and we are they and they are us.

This is how we're meant to be,
each of us one,
each of us all.

You reach out across the void of Otherness to me
and you touch your own soul!

forgiveness

Let us forgive the worst among us
because the worst is in ourselves,
the worst lives in each of us,
along with the best.

Let us forgive the worst
in each of us
and all of us
so that the best
in each of us
and all of us
may be free.

difference

Let us love not only our sameness
but our unsameness.

In our difference is our strength.

Let us be not for ourselves alone
but also for that Other

who is our deepest Self.

the message

Silence, they say, is the voice of complicity.
But silence is impossible.
Silence screams.
Silence is a message,
just as doing nothing is an act.

Let who you are ring out and resonate
in every word and every deed.
Yes, become who you are.
There's no sidestepping your own being
or your own responsibility.

What you do is who you are.
You are your own comeuppance.
You become your own message.

You are the message.

In the Spirit of Crazy Horse

The End

editor's note

As I write this, just before Christmas 1998, the U.S. Federal Penitentiary at Leavenworth, Kansas, is in a state of lockdown and I'm out of touch with author Leonard Peltier just as his book is about to go into printed proofs. The Leavenworth lockdown was apparently caused by a fight that had nothing to do with Leonard, yet he and all other inmates are being collectively punished. All personal belongings have been stripped from prisoners' cells. They've been allowed out of their locked cells only for a single ten-minute shower this past week. Just as I need him to give final approval to various details in the final edited manuscript, he's out of touch with the outside world — no visitors, no phone calls, no contact *period.* No way of knowing for the time being how he's doing or what's been happening to him. This has happened all too often over the years we've spent working on this book.

The International Office of the Leonard Peltier Defense Committee is flooding the Internet with appeals for his supporters to contact the prison — 913-682-

8700—and the Bureau of Prisons—202-307-3198, 202-514-6878 fax—to inquire about Leonard's health and safety. They have already been flooded with calls, faxes, and letters—and also threatened with a lawsuit—over the continuing denial of competent medical treatment for Leonard's jaw problems, caused by a childhood case of lockjaw and unhelped by surgery in 1996 at the Springfield Medical Facility. Rumors this past fall that prison officials would finally allow Leonard to be treated by doctors at the renowned Mayo Clinic have, as of this writing, proved groundless. We keep hoping.

Meanwhile, Leonard's case has become a centerpiece of Amnesty International's 1998–1999 focus on human rights abuses in the United States. Nonviolent civil disobedience demonstrations to publicize Leonard's case are scheduled at scores of sites around the country. President Clinton—the one person who can free Leonard with the stroke of a pen, and has had five years to do so—is under his own onslaught at this moment, one more victim of an overzealous and vindictive prosecutor.

Just recently, the European Parliament, as well as the governments of Italy and Belgium, have passed resolutions calling for clemency for Leonard Peltier as well as for Congressional investigations into the circumstances surrounding his case and the whole era of the 1970s "Reign of Terror" at Pine Ridge—and government involvement in it. Many within the Canadian government are demanding that Peltier be returned to that country, from which Peltier was fraudulently extradited by the U.S. government in 1976.

I pray that Leonard will be a free man when this book comes out in June 1999, so that we will have the privilege of hearing his own words spoken from his own lips. Although often written in pain and darkness and isolation, those words—like the incandescent spirit of this extraordinary human being—shine through every one of these pages. I want to thank Leonard for the high honor of being chosen to select, edit, arrange, and, on more than a few occasions, to goad him into revealing even deeper levels of his thought and memory.

I hope that this book, prepared under often trying circumstances for the past two years, will add to a renewed surge in public awareness that will not only help to free Leonard but will help to free us all from the kind of insidious injustice that has put him where he is—and kept him there for nearly a quarter of a century. We have all, every one of us, allowed it to happen. We must all join—yes, every one of us—and demand that it end.

If, when you read this, U.S.P. #89637-132 remains a prisoner of injustice, then the time is *now* for you, too, to speak out and for you, too, to act. Every single one of us is needed. As Leonard has said, "We must each be an army of one." To mobilize your own voice and your own conscience, contact:

Leonard Peltier Defense Committee
P.O. Box 583
Lawrence, KS 66044
785-842-5774
lpdc@idir.net

In the spirit of Leonard Peltier,
    Harvey Arden
    December 1998

appendices

appendix i

Leonard Peltier Chronology

September 12, 1944
Leonard Peltier born in Grand Forks, North Dakota, to
Leo and Alvina Peltier.

1948–53
Lives mostly with grandparents Alex and Mary Dubois-
Peltier on the Turtle Mountain Chippewa Reservation in
North Dakota.

1953–1956
Student at the BIA's Wahpeton (ND) Indian school.

1957
Finishes 9th grade at Flandreau Indian school in South
Dakota, then returns to Turtle Mountain Reservation.

1958
Troubles with the law begin: Leonard attends first Sun
Dance as an observer at Turtle Mountain; on way out,
arrested by BIA police — falsely — for being drunk. Also
arrested same year for trying to siphon diesel fuel from

223

an Army Reserve truck to heat his grandparents' home; serves two weeks in jail.

Attends a political meeting at Turtle Mountain about the government's plans to "terminate" the reservation; inspired to become a warrior on behalf of the People.

Rejected for scholarship by Santa Fe art school; drops out of school.

1959

Moves to Seattle and lives with family of cousin Bob Robideau.

1961

Given medical discharge from the Marines because of recurring problems with his jaw.

1965

Leonard and cousin Bob Robideau open an auto body shop in Seattle.

1968

American Indian Movement (AIM) established in Minneapolis.

1969

Occupation of Alcatraz by Indian activists; Leonard plays no part, but the occupation inspires his own political consciousness and provides a model for his future efforts in Indian activism.

1970
March 8

Leonard and other Indian activists occupy abandoned Fort Lawton, near Seattle — testing an old federal law that gives Indians first claim to lands abandoned by federal agencies. The activists are beaten and briefly jailed, but ultimately Fort Lawton becomes an Indian cultural center.

1972

Leonard joins AIM, moves to Pine Ridge Reservation in South Dakota, working with Dennis Banks.

Moves to Milwaukee to work with local AIM office.

That fall, Leonard joins "The Trail of Broken Treaties" caravan to Washington, D.C., to bring list of twenty grievances to the United States government. When BIA officials renege on promise to find accommodations for the Elders, the Indians stage takeover of the BIA building a few blocks from the White House just days before the 1972 presidential election. The Nixon Administration avoids violent confrontation by promising to review the list of twenty grievances (they never did) and paying the return-home expenses of the occupiers. Leonard serves on security during the takeover, becoming marked as a "troublemaker" by the FBI.

After returning to Milwaukee, Leonard is arrested and beaten when two plainclothes policemen goad him into a fight. The police claim he threatened them with a pistol—which Leonard denies—and charge him with attempted murder, even though the pistol is broken and unusable. He spends five months in jail awaiting trial while fellow AIM activists stage the famous takeover at Wounded Knee on the Pine Ridge Reservation in South Dakota. In April, friends raise bail for his release, and Leonard goes underground, fearing a kangaroo trial on the attempted murder charges (of which he would finally be acquitted in 1978). Freedom of Information Act materials released years later reveal an FBI plot to have local police arrest AIM leaders on "every possible charge."

1973

The 71-day Wounded Knee siege ends with negotiated surrender by the militants on May 9, 1973. Still, so-called GOONs continue their infamous "Reign of Terror" against Pine Ridge traditionals and their AIM supporters.

late 1973–early 1975

Although a fugitive, Leonard joins the Puyallup and Nisqually fishing rights struggle in Washington State, then takes part in AIM protests in Arizona and Wisconsin.

1975

Crescendoing "Reign of Terror" during early 1975 prompts Pine Ridge Elders to summon AIM for protection from attacks by the GOONs. Among those who respond: Leonard Peltier. He and others set up a small "tent city" on the Jumping Bull family property near Oglala, hoping to fend off further GOON attacks.

On June 26, FBI agents Jack Coler and Ronald Williams, in unmarked cars, drive at full-speed onto the Jumping Bull property, ostensibly chasing a red pickup truck in which they suspect a minor thief is riding. The FBI has never explained why it made such concerted effort to catch that thief—accused of stealing a pair of used cowboy boots—when it had failed to investigate the recent deaths of dozens of AIM supporters. A firefight erupts between the intruding unidentified agents and the AIM defenders. Within minutes, scores of FBI agents, U.S. marshals, BIA police, and trigger-happy GOONs surround the Jumping Bull property; many of them had been in place nearby at least twenty minutes before, ac-

cording to FBI documents. The two agents and one
Indian defender die during the fierce hours-long firefight. By late afternoon, Leonard and more than two
dozen others manage to flee the property and escape,
despite being surrounded by a tightening cordon of
lawmen.

Meanwhile, the leader of the tribal council signs a
secret agreement transferring one-eighth of the Pine
Ridge Reservation to the federal government—lands rich
in uranium and other minerals. Many traditionals believe
the FBI's June 26 attack was a planned diversion to conceal the land transfer—a diversion that went terribly
wrong when their agents were killed.

Following the escape of Leonard and the others from
the Jumping Bull property, the FBI stages a massive manhunt for the escapees, terrorizing the Pine Ridge traditional community.

Leonard secretly attends Crow Dog's Sun Dance in
August, then heads north and west, escaping across the
Canadian border and winning refuge with a remote
group of Indians in the Rockies.

September 5

In the midst of a new flurry of unexplained murders of
AIM members, the FBI raids the home of medicine man
Leonard Crow Dog, spiritual leader of the Wounded
Knee takeover, and arrests Darrell "Dino" Butler—
another AIM escapee from the Oglala firefight—along
with Crow Dog himself and AIM activist Anna Mae
Aquash. Neither of the latter were at the Oglala firefight. According to Aquash, an FBI agent threatens her
with death unless she gives false testimony against Peltier
and others from AIM; she refuses.

September 10

A station wagon driven by Bob Robideau, another fleeing escapee, explodes near Wichita, Kansas. From the wreck the FBI recovers a badly burned AR-15 rifle—claiming without any proof whatsoever (1) that it was the weapon that killed the agents and (2) that it was Leonard Peltier's own rifle. This weapon and the casings supposedly from it were among the key evidence later used against Leonard in his trial.

October

FBI lab reports—not revealed until they were obtained years later through the Freedom of Information Act—state that the Witchita AR-15 rifle "contains a different pin than the rifle used at the Jumping Bull scene," thus flatly disproving that the Witchita rifle was the murder weapon. This and other pieces of crucial exculpatory evidence were hidden away by the prosecution and withheld from the defense at Leonard's later trial in Fargo.

November 25

Four men are indicted by a federal grand jury for their alleged role in the deaths of the two FBI agents. The four are Leonard Peltier, Bob Robideau, Dino Butler, and Jimmy Eagle (the man suspected of stealing the piar of cowboy boots whose theft allegedly brought the two FBI agents to the Jumping Bull property the day of the firefight).

1976

February 6

Peltier arrested by the Royal Canadian Mounted Police in western Canada. He is held under maximum security at Oakalla Prison in Vancouver, B.C., while lengthy extradition hearings are held.

228

February 10

FBI releases a report stating that it had found a match between the Witchita AR-15 rifle and a .223 rifle-shell casing found, belatedly, in the trunk of one of the FBI agents' cars. This totally contradicts their own earlier lab reports, which they kept hidden.

February 24

Decomposed body of a "Jane Doe" is found in a gulley on Pine Ridge; BIA coroner reports the victim died of exposure to cold; her hands are cut off and taken by FBI for "positive identification."

March 5

"Jane Doe" identified by FBI as Anna Mae Aquash, AIM activist who had refused, despite FBI death threats, to give false testimony against her AIM brothers and sisters.

March 11

Anna Mae Aquash's family from the MicMac Reservation in Nova Scotia has her body exhumed from Pine Ridge burial. A new coroner discovers a detail the BIA coroner had unaccountably missed: she had been shot in the back of the head at close range. Her death, shortly before her expected appearance at upcoming trials of Peltier and the others, leaves a mystery being actively explored to this day. Anna Mae seemed to have foreseen her own demise when she wrote:

> *"I'm Indian all the way, and always will be. I'm not going to stop fighting til I die, and hope I'm a good example of a human being and of my tribe . . . I have a right to continue my cycle in this Universe undisturbed . . . I'll talk to you through the rain . . ."*

March 31

Still trying to find convincing evidence of Peltier's guilt so as to gain his extradition from Canada, FBI agents show photographs of Anna Mae's severed hands to a confused Indian woman, Myrtle Poor Bear, telling her both she and her daughter faced a similar fate unless she co-operated. Under duress, she signs an affadavit they wrote for her stating that she is Peltier's girlfriend — though she had never met him — and also claims she saw him shoot the agents — though, as the FBI knew, she was never there. This affadavit and other fabricated information convince the Canadian courts there is enough evidence to extradite Peltier; he is ordered extradited but his appeals keep him in Canada until December.

June 7–July 16

Trial of Dino Butler and Bob Robideau in Cedar Rapids, Iowa. Allowed to plead innocent by reason of self-defense in firing at the intruding FBI agents, Butler and Robideau win full acquittal on murder charges after a tumultuous trial.

Dismayed by the results of the Cedar Rapids trial, the FBI and prosecutors drop charges against Jimmy Eagle so that, as FOIA documents would later reveal, "the full prosecutive weight of the Federal government could be directed against Leonard Peltier."

December 16

Peltier extradited from Canada to the U.S. on the basis of false testimony fabricated by the FBI. Under massive security, he is flown from Vancouver to Rapid City, South Dakota.

1977
March 16

Trial of Leonard Peltier on double murder charges begins in Fargo, North Dakota. Government manipulations transfer the trial from Cedar Rapids, Iowa, where Robideau and Butler were acquitted, to a site renowned for anti-Indian sentiment. The Fargo judge rules all evidence must be tightly limited to events of the day of the shootout: June 26, 1975. No mention is allowed of the "Reign of Terror" preceding the shootout at Pine Ridge, nor of Myrtle Poor Bear's false affadavit, nor of FBI intimidation and coercion of witnesses, nor of most of the evidence that had led to the acquittal by reason of self-defense of Robideau and Butler at Cedar Rapids. Judge declares: "The FBI is not on trial here." Peltier not permitted to claim "self-defense." In a shocking and flagrant display of American injustice, virtually all exculpatory evidence is hidden from the defense or ruled inadmissable.

April 18

Under an extraordinary kangaroo-court atmosphere of intimidation by the government, an all-white jury, after eight hours of deliberation, convicts Peltier of the direct murder of the two FBI agents.

June 2

Peltier sentenced to two consecutive life terms in federal prison. After a stint at Leavenworth, he's sent to Marion Maximum-Security Penitentiary in Illinois.

1978
July 4

Peltier warned by fellow Native inmate that he will soon be transferred from Marion Maximum-Security Penitentiary to Lompoc prison near Santa Barbara, California, where, he's told, he will be the target of an assassination.

1979
March 5

U.S. Supreme Court refuses to review Leonard's case.

April 10

Peltier transferred to Lompoc prison, as he had been warned.

July 20

Fearing an imminent assassination attempt, Peltier — with fellow Native prisoners Dallas Thundershield and Bobby Garcia — climbs over perimeter fence and escapes from Lompoc prison. Dallas Thundershield is shot in back and killed. Bobby Garcia quickly recaptured, but Peltier escapes and eludes huge manhunt until finally recaptured in a farmer's field five days later. At subsequent trial for the escape, he was not allowed to use fear of assassination as a defense. Seven years added to original double-life sentence.

1980
February 4

Leonard transferred back to Marion Maximum-Security Penitentiary. He now believes the whole Lompoc "assassination" story was a set-up to get him to attempt an escape, giving guards an excuse to kill him.

December 13

Bobby Garcia found dead in prison facility at Terre Haute Federal Penitentiary. Authorities claim he hanged himself. Many are convinced he was murdered.

1984
October 1

Hearings for a new trial begin in Bismark, N.D., before the same judge who presided at Leonard's Fargo trial.

1985
May 22

Even though original prosecutor admits government doesn't know who killed the FBI agents, the same judge denies Leonard's appeal for a new trial.

June

Leonard transferred to Leavenworth prison in Kansas.

1986
September 11

Peltier's conviction affirmed by U.S. 8th Circuit Court of Appeals, despite acknowledgment of FBI misconduct.

1991
April 18

Senior Judge Gerald Heaney of the 8th Circuit panel that denied Leonard's 1986 appeal, now—having left the Court—writes to the president that evidence of unlawful misconduct by the FBI and other governmental agencies before, during, and after the Fargo trial persuades him that Leonard deserves executive clemency.

July 5

Riot at Leavenworth. Leonard at first charged as "active participant," even though he had only tried to get Native inmates away from the fray. He was later cleared in the incident, but not before serving a stretch in the Hole.

1991
October

Evidentiary hearing for a new trial held in Bismarck, N.D.

233

December 30

Petition for new trial denied again by original judge at 1977 Fargo trial.

1992
March 23

Leonard's attorneys file a new appeal with the 8th Circuit Court of Appeals.

November 9

Original prosecutor at Fargo trial admits again before 8th Circuit Court that the government doesn't know who killed the two agents.

1993
July 7

Despite overwhelming exculpatory evidence, the 8th Circuit Court again denies Leonard's appeal and reaffirms his conviction.

1993
November 21

After U.S. Parole Commission denies appeal for parole, Leonard's appeals attorney, Ramsey Clark, formally petitions for executive clemency from the president; application sent to attorney general for review and recommendation, a process normally taking from three to nine months.

1995
February 6

Leonard begins 20th year in prison — measured from his arrest in Canada on February 6, 1976.

December

Leonard temporarily transferred to U.S. Medical Center

for federal prisoners in Springfield, Missouri, for surgery
on his ailing jaw; requires six blood transfusions, nearly
dies.

1996
March 19

U.S. Parole Commission again denies parole to Leonard;
tells him to reapply in the year 2008.

1998
May 4

At an interim parole hearing, the U.S. Parole Commission reaffirms its denial of parole for Leonard; again tells
him to reapply in year 2008.

September 12

Leonard's 54th birthday; in prison since age 31.

November 21

Five years after petition was made, Leonard's appeal for
clemency remains mired in the attorney general's office.

December 19

National day of nonviolent civil disobedience focuses on
the government's long delay in responding to executive
clemency plea.

1999
February 6

Leonard begins his 24th year in prison.

appendix ii

I've come to hate courtrooms because they seem too often the home not of justice but of injustice. Overzealous prosecutors prey on the innocent and the guilty alike. "Getting their man" is more important than finding the truth, much less finding justice, demonstrating wisdom, or showing human compassion. Unknowing and misinformed juries are tricked, or even bullied, into unjust decisions. Officers of the law, from police to judges, knowingly connive to subvert the truth as often as they selectively uphold it. Ever more prisons await those caught in this unholy system, whether they're guilty or innocent, and within those cold and inhuman walls and circling razor-wire fences the punishment and the injustice will be continued, even multiplied with a vengeance, as if the loss of one's freedom were not punishment enough. To those of you who see the cure to America's ills in building more prisons, I beg you—rethink what you are doing. Maybe you can sweep the streets of all undesirables, of everyone who is an Other, but one of these days, my friend, you may be declared Other yourself—and then you'll find that one of those new and shiny cells you paid your taxes for was built just for you.

I want to include here my pre-sentencing address to the presiding judge following the Fargo trial. I know these are harsh words, but they are true to the core. The only response from the judge, before he sentenced me to two life terms, was, "You profess to be an activist for your people, but you are a disservice to Native Americans." I will let you — and history — decide who spoke the truth that dark day in the history of American injustice.

—L. P.

Pre-Sentencing Statement by Leonard Peltier Fargo, North Dakota, June 1, 1977

"There's no doubt in my mind or my people's minds you are going to sentence me to two consecutive life terms. You are, and always have been, prejudiced against me and any Native Americans who have stood before you. You have openly favored the government all through this trial, and you are happy to do whatever the FBI would want you to do in this case.

"I did not always believe this to be so. When I first saw you in the courtroom in Sioux Falls, your dignified appearance misled me into thinking that you were a fairminded person who knew something of the law, and who would act in accordance with the law. Which meant that you would be impartial and not favor one side or the other in this lawsuit. That hasn't been the case, and I now firmly believe that you will impose consecutive life terms solely because that way you think you will avoid the displeasure of the FBI. Yet neither my people nor myself know why you would be so concerned about an organization that has brought so much shame to the American people. But you are! Your conduct during this trial leaves no doubt that you will do the bidding of the FBI without any hesitation.

"You are about to perform an act which will close one more chapter in the history of the failure of the United States to do justice in the case of a Native American. After centuries of murder of millions of my brothers and sisters by white racist America, could I have been wise in thinking you would break that tradition and commit an act of justice? Obviously not. Because I should have realized that what I detected was only a very thin layer of dignity and surely not of fine character.

"If you think my accusations have been harsh and unfounded, I will explain why I have reached these conclusions, and why I think my criticism has not been harsh enough.

"First: Each time my defense tried to expose FBI misconduct in their investigation of this lawsuit . . . and tried to present evidence of this, you claimed it was irrelevant to this trial. But the prosecution was allowed to present their case with evidence that was in no way relevant to this lawsuit. For example, an automobile blowing up on a freeway in Wichita, Kansas; an attempted murder in Milwaukee, Wisconsin, for which I have not been found innocent or guilty; or a van loaded with legally sold firearms and a policeman who claims someone fired at him in Oregon State.

"The Supreme Court of the United States tried to prevent convictions of this sort by passing into law that only past convictions may be presented as evidence. . . . This court knows very well I have no prior convictions, nor am I even charged with some of those alleged crimes. Therefore, they cannot be used as evidence in order to receive a conviction in this farce called a trial. This is why I strongly believe you will impose two life terms, running consecutively, on me.

238

"Second: You could not make a reasonable decision about my sentence because you suffer from at least one of three defects that prevent a rational conclusion. You plainly demonstrated this in your decision about the Jimmy Eagle and Myrtle Poor Bear aspects of this case. In Jimmy's case, for some unfounded reason that only a judge who consciously ignores the law would call irrelevant to my trial. In the mental torture of Myrtle Poor Bear, you said her testimony would shock the conscience of the American people if believed! But you decided what was to be believed, not the jury! Your conduct shocks the conscience of what the American system stands for—the search for the truth by a jury of citizens. What was it that made you so afraid to let that testimony in? Your own guilt of being part of a corrupt, preplanned trial to get a conviction no matter how your reputation would be tarnished? For these reasons I strongly believe you will do the bidding of the FBI and give me two consecutive life terms.

"Third: In my opinion, anyone who failed to see the relationship between the undisputed facts of these events surrounding the investigation used by the FBI in their interrogation of the Navajo youths—Wilford Draper, who was tied to a chair for three hours and denied access to his attorney; the outright threats to Norman Brown's life; the bodily harm threatened to Mike Anderson; and finally, the murder of Anna Mae Aquash—must be blind, stupid, or without human feelings. So there is no doubt, and little chance, that you have the ability to avoid doing today what the FBI wants you to do, which is to sentence me to two life terms consecutively.

"Fourth: You do not have the ability to see that the conviction of an AIM activist helps to cover up what the government's own evidence showed—that a large number of Indian people was engaged in that firefight on June 26,

239

1975. You do not have the ability to see that the government must suppress the fact that there is a growing anger among Indian people and that Native Americans will resist any further encroachments by the military forces of the capitalistic Americans, which is evidenced by the large number of Pine Ridge residents who took up arms on June 26, 1975, to defend themselves. Therefore, you do not have the ability to carry out your responsibility towards me in an impartial way, and you will run my two life terms consecutively.

"Fifth: I stand before you as a proud man. I feel no guilt. I have done nothing to feel guilty about! I have no regrets of being a Native American activist. Thousands of people in the United States, Canada, and around the world have and will continue to support me to expose the injustices which have occurred in this courtroom. I do feel pity for your people that they must live under such an ugly system. Under your system you are taught greed, racism, corruption — and, most serious of all, the destruction of Mother Earth. Under the Native American system, we are taught all people are brothers and sisters, and to share the wealth with the poor and needy. But the most important of all is to respect and preserve the Earth, whom we consider to be our Mother. We feed from her breast. Our Mother gives us life from birth, and, when it's time to leave this world, she takes us back again into her womb. But the main thing we are taught is to preserve her for our children and our grandchildren — because they are the next who will live upon her.

"No, I'm not the guilty one here. I'm not the one who should be called a criminal. White racist America is the criminal for the destruction of our lands and my people. To hide your guilt from the decent human beings in America and around the world, you will sentence me to two life terms without hesitation.

"Sixth: There are less than four hundred federal judges

for a population of over two hundred million Americans. Therefore, you have a very powerful and important responsibility, which should be carried out impartially. But you have never been impartial where I was concerned. You have the responsibility of protecting constitutional rights and laws, but, where I was concerned, you neglected to even consider my or Native Americans' constitutional rights. But, most important of all, you neglected our human rights!

"If you were impartial you would have had an open mind on all the factual disputes in this case. But you were unwilling to allow even the slightest possibility that a law officer would lie on the stand. Then how could you possibly be impartial enough to let my lawyers prove how important it is to the FBI to convict a Native American activist in this case? You do not have the ability to see that such a conviction is an important part of the efforts to discredit those who are trying to alert their brothers and sisters to the new threat from the white man, and the attempt to destroy what little Indian land remains in the process of extracting our uranium, oil, and other minerals. Again — to cover up your part in this — you will call me heartless, a coldblooded murderer who deserves two life sentences consecutively.

"Seventh: I cannot expect a judge who has openly tolerated the conditions I have been jailed under to make an impartial decision on whether I should be sentenced to concurrent or consecutive life terms. You have been made aware of the following conditions which I had to endure at the Grand Forks County jail, since the time of the verdict: (1) I was denied access to a phone to call my attorneys concerning my appeal; (2) I was locked in solitary confinement without shower facilities, soap, towels, sheets, or pillow; (3) the food was inedible, what little there was of it; (4) my family — brothers, sisters, mother and father, who traveled long distances from the reservation — was denied visitation.

241

"No human being should be subjected to such treatment. . . . Again, the only conclusion that comes to mind is that you know and always knew you would sentence me to two consecutive life terms.

"Finally, I honestly believe you made up your mind long ago that I was guilty and that you were going to sentence me to the maximum sentence permitted under the law. But this doesn't surprise me, because you are a high-ranking member of the white racist American Establishment, which consistently said 'In God We Trust' while they went about the business of murdering my people and attempting to destroy our culture.

"The only thing I'm guilty of, and which I was convicted for, was being of Chippewa and Sioux blood — and for believing in our sacred religion."

The judge then sentenced me to two consecutive life terms. His own day of judgment, I believe, will be held in a higher court.

I will add here just a few more words I spoke to the 8th Court of Appeals after the Court, despite mountains of exculpatory evidence, refused to grant me a new trial in 1986.

"I spoke out for many years against the injustices Native people suffer before they sent me into prison for speaking out and organizing against the human rights violations of our Mother Earth. I have not stopped speaking out just because my body has been locked away. . . . This vocal opposition and my organizing work are the real reason they have put me in prison.

"I firmly believe even the FBI and the U.S. prosecutors who have worked on this case know I am not guilty of aiding and abetting murder. I have never advocated violence. I have never used violence."

And I never will.

—Leonard Peltier